I am very proud of my brother for writing this book. I've always said you heal as you reveal, and this book expresses his experiences regarding his faith walk honestly, and in humility. If you want to understand how to transform your life experiences into a personal catalyst for your growth, look no further.

Kirk Franklin

The layers of Lecrae's writings stretch down below the surface where most of us tend to live. His work does what good books and music should—require a reckoning for individuals like us, for the churches we attend, and for whole communities, like the ones we live in. With the staggering transparency that we've come to respect him for, Lecrae writes about his wrestling and brings his whole soul to bear in the pages that you are holding in your hands. Then, with unapologetic clarity, he points toward real solutions for the toxic circumstances we've been running from our whole lives. He poses the questions we've been too busy or too disinterested or too inarticulate to ask, and then he unearths perspective and insights we've been too myopic to clearly see. This book helps us. It has helped me. Write on, Lecrae. Your words are healing us.

Priscilla Shirer, Bible teacher and *New York Times* bestselling author

Our world is desperate to learn how a true trailblazer like Lecrae manages to keep living, loving, and creating amid personal and cultural chaos. This book is a beacon of light for anyone wanting to live a life of true impact and significance. If that's you, read this book and follow Lecrae's lead.

Joel Marion, bestselling author, cofounder of BioTrust Nutrition, and host of the *Born to Impact* podcast

Lecrae has an incredible capacity to inspire those around him in everything he does: his music, his conversations, his friendship, his writings, his lifestyle. Nowhere is that more obvious than in his book I *Am Restored*. It is a powerful, authentic story, not just of the trauma that invades our lives but of the strength and life that

God gives us amid the chaos. His story is at times heartbreaking, but always filled with hope—and that is why it will resonate so strongly with anyone who reads it.

Judah Smith, lead pastor of Churchome

There is always a powerful story behind any great artist. Lecrae shares his personal journey of challenges and victories with honesty and hope in his book I Am Restored. You will be encouraged and inspired by the life he continues to live out loud for the glory of Jesus.

Rich Wilkerson, lead pastor of VOUS Church

Lecrae continues to inspire and influence millions through his bestselling albums and books, and now he has delivered again with his new book, I Am Restored, as he details his journey like never before, reflecting on his personal tragedies and triumphs, and the lessons he has learned while walking on the road to restoration with God. If you're looking to be filled with hope and encouragement as you journey with God, then this is a must-read book for you.

Albert Tate, founding pastor of Fellowship Church

Sharing the facts of an event is one matter. Sharing how those facts have shaped the arc of your life and the need to be made whole from them is another. This is true vulnerability. In our culture, particularly for men, this measure of being exposed ranges from rare to nonexistent. Yet, herein my brother Lecrae lays himself bare, revealing before us a man willing—after what is often the most arduous journey of navigating our own internal world and associated traumas—to be truly seen. Laying aside "celebrity," "reputation," and self-protection, he does, through his story, invite us to do the same—to be truly seen. It is only when we have faced ourselves and taken all before Him who heals that we can truly experience restoration. I am so grateful for the signposts and path Lecrae has laid before us all.

Pastor Léonce B. Crump Jr., author, Renovate: Changing Who You Are by Loving Where You Are, founder of Renovation Church

I AM
RESTORED

I AM RESTORED

HOW I LOST MY RELIGION
BUT FOUND MY FAITH

LECRAE

WITH TYLER BURNS

ZONDERVAN
BOOKS

ZONDERVAN BOOKS

I Am Restored
Copyright © 2020 by Lecrae Moore

Requests for information should be addressed to:
Zondervan, 3900 Sparks Dr. SE, Grand Rapids, Michigan 49546

Zondervan titles may be purchased in bulk for educational, business,
fundraising, or sales promotional use. For information, please email
SpecialMarkets@Zondervan.com.

ISBN 978-0-310-35803-9 (hardcover)
ISBN 978-0-310-35805-3 (audio)
ISBN 978-0-310-35804-6 (ebook)

Cover design: Alex Medina
Cover image: Alex Harper
Interior design: Denise Froehlich

Printed in the United States of America

20 21 22 23 24 /LSC/ 10 9 8 7 6 5 4 3 2 1

Dedication

Thank you to all the women who have poured into my life. Boys need fathers, but you women stepped in and wrapped your arms around me in wondrous ways. Big Mama, Mom, Granna, aunties, cousins . . . I love you. God sent you into my life. Darragh, only God could give you the strength you need to wrestle with the likes of me. Your grace, love, and wisdom have made me stronger.

Contents

PART 1

FACING MY OWN CHAOS

CHAPTER 1

My Childhood Wounds

At the end of my book *Unashamed*,[1] I had arrived. Well, not really, but that's probably what some people believed when they read it. Maybe it's how I felt when I wrote it. It's easy to hear the story of that period of my life and believe that I had reached the pinnacle of my life and career. Sure, I had experienced life difficulties during my childhood and stared down the reality of abuse. I had encountered critics and detractors from my attempts to adjust who I was reaching with my artistry. I hadn't fully faced myself yet.

I had answered questions about my ministry authenticity and artistic legitimacy, or so I thought. My songs were being played on mainstream radio stations. I had connections in the very spheres I felt I had been called to. I had won countless awards, peaking with a coveted Grammy. I had it all, right?

....
1 Lecrae, with Jonathan Merritt, *Unashamed* (Nashville: B&H, 2016).

That's how it looked from the outside. By all accounts, I was doing well, at the top of my game and ready to reach new heights. Even those who have been to the "peak" of their professions gave me acknowledgment and respect. But something was happening. An uncomfortable shift was taking place in my life and threatened to derail all the greatness I had achieved. All the awards and accolades can't hide the weaknesses of the heart.

I was broken. No, I still am broken. We always talk about our brokenness with a small measure of authenticity but as though it were something far-off that doesn't affect our families, our marriages, our well-being. The great lie of dysfunction is that things are "not that bad." Sure, I had respectable addictions to substances and pleasure. But I'm "managing." Yes, my relationship with my wife is in shambles, but don't worry—I'm "working on it." No, I haven't had a meaningful interaction with my children in months, but "I'll figure it out." I did not realize it yet, but dysfunction was subtly luring me into a pit of chaos, chipping away at my God-given purpose piece by piece.

You might be reading this book and expecting me to give you some clichés, to reference some of your favorite Scriptures out of context to tell you I overcame with sheer will and tenacity. If that's what you are anticipating me to say, I'm sorry to disappoint you. I have left that assumption of perfection behind. I am unwilling to act like I have all the answers just to preserve your perception of my celebrity.

It's easy for people to believe the myth that celebrity means healthy. But in our time there are many examples that contradict that myth. Many celebrities, comedians, artists, politicians, and tastemakers have fallen to an inner turmoil and darkness that they couldn't overcome. The greatest voices have lost their will to speak. The most competent moral representatives have failed to maintain the standard they set for others. The most joyful people have drowned in a pool of despair. In the end, regardless of our popularity and professional status, we are only human.

Part of the difficulty of being a public figure is people not recognizing your humanity. Actually, the more dangerous part of being a public figure for me was not recognizing my own humanity. It's easy to point the finger at others, but I lost sight of myself. We are not immune to the crushing pain of our own human failings. No matter how successful we become, when the lights go off, we are forced to live with ourselves. Career achievement didn't protect Heath Ledger from the pain. Money and fame didn't insulate Robin Williams or Anthony Bourdain. It didn't protect Kate Spade or Don Cornelius. I read their stories, watched the collective trauma of their pain, and realized that there was something wrong with me too.

On the inside, deep turmoil was brewing in my soul, a restlessness that's hard to describe. I pushed it away for days, then weeks, then months and years. I suppressed my feelings of anguish because I was convinced I wasn't allowed to be vulnerable; or maybe it was because I convinced myself of lies that would soon unravel right in front of me. Whatever it was, a wall was quickly approaching, and I wouldn't be able to dodge it.

What makes a person healthy? What is the true meaning of being whole and complete as a human being? Some would say that it's all found in the way someone expresses their faith or their theology. Others would argue that health is a by-product of our physical conditioning and discipline. Experts in other fields might say that it's how closely we've achieved our goals and lived in our purpose.

I thought I had all that. I believed that my theology and methodology were correct and above heresy. I believed I had enough discipline to last a lifetime, and I had already achieved countless goals I had set for myself. So what was missing? I still wasn't healthy.

My soul was deeply disturbed. I slowly began to realize that I was facing something that I had failed to address with the right amount of fervor. I was dealing with trauma. In all my years of learning about theology, church, and the Bible, I hadn't heard anything about trauma or its effect on the human body, even though countless biblical characters clearly struggled with melancholy or depression. Elijah, David, and even Jesus wrestled with inner pain that drove them to their knees.

Recently I read a book called *The Body Keeps the Score*. In it Dr. Bessel van der Kolk writes about this reality, saying, "The essence of trauma is that it is overwhelming, unbelievable, and unbearable."[2] That's exactly how I felt. He adds, "As long as you keep secrets and suppress information, you are

....

2 Bessel A. van der Kolk, *The Body Keeps the Score: Brain, Mind, and Body in the Healing of Trauma* (New York: Penguin, 2014), 197.

fundamentally at war with yourself."[3] I felt like I was at war with myself too.

I was drowning in the chaos.

A few years ago, at the height of my career and the peak of my influence, I paused to look at my life and saw that it was in disarray. Initially I didn't want to overreact from where I was in that moment. Sometimes we have seasons of struggle or lapses in judgment that shift our life from happy and whole to complicated and stressed. Those seasons weren't unusual for me. But my assessment of chaos had little to do with a season of life. The turmoil began long before I identified it, like a virus slowly infecting every area of my life. I was caught up in a cycle of self-destruction that threatened to sabotage everything I had worked hard to create.

My "struggles," as we like to call them, weren't just difficult circumstances or "trials" that we talk about in church services. My life was a wreck. I was a sickly mashup of addiction and self-medication. My vibrant and passionate commitment to being present for my family was now inconsistent at best. At first I just felt "off," but then I had a few episodes of problematic behavior, and that quickly sank into a spiral of anguish that I thought I would never escape from.

But I'm Lecrae. Thousands of people look to me for guidance. They see me as a leader of a movement. Sure, I can have "struggles" (whatever that means in our Christian celebrity spaces). I could even have "trials." That would make for inspiring lyrics on a new album and a provocative press tour.

....
3 Kolk, *Body Keeps the Score*, 235.

But chaos? I can't have a life filled with chaos. I can't. I was terrified that people would find out that I was a fraud, someone who was just as flawed and human as they are.

Another part of me was just lost. I fluctuated between caring deeply about what everyone would think of me to refusing to care at all. In those moments I didn't even care what people or fans thought; I just wanted to be free from the pain I was trapped in. I was hurting and needed someone to show me the way out.

In the middle of all this pain, I realized that I didn't have the right "Christian" response to find the escape from my trial. This was probably the most haunting, hopeless part of my journey. The obvious remedies you always hear from fellow believers—"Just pray about it!" "Let go and let God!" "Well, maybe you should just worship God more and read your Bible!"—weren't reaching my soul. Something was missing.

I had no answers for how to escape my chaos and find healing. I didn't have a collection of Bible verses that would help me understand exactly what was happening or how I could experience true freedom. I felt stuck.

I finally discovered that I wasn't alone. Talking to my friends about my chaos led me to realize that many Christians operate in a functional state of chaotic living that has them bound and trapped in unhealthy patterns and habits without addressing deep root issues. We come to church every weekend and realize that a service is just a balm for the week, not a solution that gets to the root of our problems.

Most of the theology I learned was missing the right

categories for handling trauma in a healthy way. It only interacted with trauma when it was time to redeem it for the glory of God. But how do I live as a healthy human being? How do I handle trauma in a way that actually closes the loop of chaos in my life? How do I maintain honesty when even Christians cannot seem to handle the weight of my authenticity?

How is my traumatic history affecting and infecting what I do even as a grown man? How can I claim to be a follower of Jesus and an artist who represents him if my life is so broken?

The Christian response to pain is often characterized by three different approaches. Some Christians want to minimize pain. They try to pass over it quickly and move on to other concerns more worth their time. Like when people ask, "How are you doing?" but don't want to hear the real answer. "I'm depressed, actually" would stun them into silence.

Christians have a disturbing habit of minimizing pain and making it seem less important than other concerns we should be focusing on. Entire movements of the church are dedicated to thinking positively about all of life and refusing to sit in pain for any length of time. But if I minimize my pain, how can I get past it? If I dismiss my suffering, how can it be redeemed?

Other Christians seek to overspiritualize pain. If God is good, what purpose is there in meditating on pain? They take Scriptures like "Be anxious for nothing" as proof that we're not even supposed to acknowledge the presence of anxiety and the roots of our trauma. After all, if we just "keep our minds on things above," the realities of life won't even phase us, even if they are difficult. So they say.

They boldly proclaim clichés like "God is going to work everything out for our good anyway," and "Remember this body is going to fade away anyway." In the end none of our issues will matter, so what purpose is there in even worrying deeply about them? Just quote Scriptures and remember who you are in Christ, right? How can I remember who I am in Christ if I don't have the pathway to figure out who I am?

Another group of Christians seek to memorialize pain. They construct entire theologies that are rooted not in addressing pain but in obsessing about its reality. Even though I know firsthand that pain is real and was manifesting itself in my life, to sit in that pain without resolution would just be to make the pain that much greater.

Is there any hope for me? Is there any pathway for me to keep my faith in Jesus and be healthy? I was wrestling with these questions, and I wasn't winning.

My chaos was eroding any signs of the healthy me. I learned to recognize myself in my flawed state and treat it as my default setting. I was coping with a number of addictions that I couldn't find my way free from. I knew it was wrong, but I was in pain. When I wanted to feel numb to all the anguish, I couldn't put down the bottle. I was drinking every night just to disengage from the depressive state. I wanted to mute my anxiety, to push it down as far as possible. It's one thing to have a few drinks, but I couldn't stop there. I went from functioning buzzed to getting full-blown drunk with frightening ease. When the depression was at its height, I would drink incessantly, not even worrying about what the consequences would be.

When alcohol wouldn't work, I turned to pills. The pills were supposed to help alleviate the symptoms of depression and anxiety. They were designed to make me feel better, but that wasn't working. I was popping the pills like candy, thinking they would stop the conflict in my mind. I would have bursts of hedonism, temporarily giving myself to all the forbidden fruits of my platform. At times a mixture of the pills and alcohol led to a severe lack of judgment and numbness.

These were just the tip of the iceberg. My family and friends could see the dark cloud emerging over my head that had hovered over my soul for years. A cloud of chaos.

Where does chaos come from? In some instances we are confronted with the consequences of our own chaotic decisions. We love to follow our own way, and that inevitably gets us into trouble. In other cases the only explanation for our chaotic situation is the broken nature of the world we live in. Sometimes circumstances happen outside our control or understanding. But most of us regularly fail to acknowledge the third source of chaos: the sins of others.

When I realized I was in the midst of my free fall, I knew that some of my own decisions created the foundation for the chaos in my life. That part was obvious. I was taught early in my walk with Jesus to examine myself first and see all the ways that my decisions were the cause of my situation.

I tried that introspection but couldn't get to the root of why I wanted to do any of the negative things I was doing. I had everything I thought I wanted: the acceptance of others, fame, success, family, and so on. Why would I want to sabotage my reality? As a "self-made" man, I had to come to grips with how the sins of others had created decades of trauma that placed me on the pathway to chaos.

I don't mean that I played no part in my chaos or that others are the sole reason why I made a mess of my life. I've never been one to blame others for the things I can control. I only mean that I didn't understand how the context of my past led me to the choices of my present. I didn't understand how much I was a product of the conditioning of my environment. I was challenged by specialists and friends to interrogate my past, to take a more honest look at my childhood. It took me back to a dark place, a place I thought I had overcome.

I remember how I felt immediately after she abused me. My body felt numb. Shallow breaths echoed throughout the pitch-black room as I sat on my bed looking down in shame. I kept glancing back and forth, as though I could find my innocence in the darkness. *What just happened?* . . . *Should I tell anyone? That was . . . a lot. Exciting? Weird?* I lay down in an attempt to process the rapid firing of all my senses. *Why did she do that? What is this feeling?* In that one moment, I was violated by a relative, someone who was assigned to care for me while my mother was away. I was taken advantage of and no longer innocent. It would be easy for me to say that I felt dirty or that I knew this was wrong, but in that moment I'm not sure that I did. I was a kid without the proper categories for what was moral or right. Plus, there was no father to vent to, no safe space where I could freely speak my truth or even ask questions.

After this experience, my sense of what intimacy was obviously was more twisted than it should have been. I grew up quickly, too quickly. And without those transparent spaces to share my truth, I lashed out with outbursts of anger, distrust, and depression. These were my ways of dealing with deep inner pain that was suffocating me from the inside out. The depth of chaos this experience created has only recently become clear to me. I had to fully face it to realize that my body and my mind were still taking me back to those moments, even as an adult.

For years I kept my abusive experiences firmly in the past. "Yeah, it happened . . . but it doesn't bother me," I'd say. Part of my strategy was trying to hide from the pain of abuse, but another part was avoiding talking about something that I didn't have the categories to address. How could I address it? I treated my pain like it could be locked tightly in a box or hidden deep in the closet of my soul. "It doesn't bother me," I would say to people who knew. But it affected me more than it bothered me, creating decades of unresolved trauma, causing a ripple effect of chaos below the surface. I could hide it for only so long.

Growing up, if you experienced sexual assault, that was seen as a joke for our "boys," a badge of honor that we would share to prove our manhood: *Look what I've done.* It's not really shameful to be molested by a woman in our culture. In a sexist world, these were bragging rights for young men to share in private moments. I took the experience to heart, believing that this was how I should act on a regular basis.

The experience of some survivors leads them to a feeling of internal judgment. They blame themselves because they didn't stop the abuse or prevent their abuser from taking advantage of their bodies. Shame forces them into silence about how abuse affects their lives. Abuse can create a blockade, preventing the healing they desperately need, all because they blame themselves for what happened. I remember hearing Dr. Christina Edmondson, a dean at Calvin College, say, "Dysfunction, sin, and trauma thrive in darkness, silence, and minimization."

My experience was different from others. I was silent about my abuse, but I didn't necessarily feel it was wrong. I wanted to feel that rush of pleasure all the time. I started having sexual experiences with friends and neighbors as early as the second grade. I let the distortion of that experience shape my humanity, my body, my soul. When you are exposed to sexuality that early without healthy categories, trauma is free to run your life.

To some this will be a startling revelation. After all, I've spoken about my sexual abuse before, sharing my heart in various formats, such as music and interview segments. The most famous example of this was the song "Good, Bad, Ugly." This was the first time I revealed my abuse in detail. I even shared more thoughts in my first book, *Unashamed.* Each time

I gave the circumstances surrounding my molestation, I was applauded for being vulnerable. "Wow, Lecrae is brave! A true leader!" In the case of the song, I was transparent for three minutes and twenty-nine seconds.

It is true that a survivor sharing their story is a powerful moment of freedom that they are not required to share. Most people can't comprehend how significant it is when survivors, especially Black men, share their stories. But my vulnerability was hollow. I only shared what happened because I assumed it would be liberating for my audience. Sharing my story was for the benefit of others rather than for my own personal healing.

Healing. For years, I never even knew what that felt like. I was a public figure, a professional artist, a record label owner, a husband, a father, the leader of a movement, and yet I didn't know what it felt like to walk in healing. The message of the gospel is that God is in the process of healing our brokenness, redeeming our scars. And I believed it and walked like it was already realized. *I'm healed!* On the outside I was looked up to as an example of strength. I accomplished most of my goals at a young age. I was on national television with the highest awards and notoriety. But internally I was broken, the kind of brokenness that slowly unravels rather than shattering in an instant. Most of my fans didn't know. Only the closest friends and family members got a front-row seat to my self-destruction. I was perpetuating a cycle of numbness to hide the weight of my trauma.

I realized that I didn't fully understand the consequence of what my abuser took from me. When speaking with survivors, most people focus on the action of abuse but not on how we should live with the pain and shame. People who are unaffected by abuse have never had to think about having to function at a high level even while they're hurting or triggered.

Experts always say a child should develop natural coping skills, but there was nothing I could do to cope with this kind of abuse. In the aftermath of my molestation, I felt all my emotions at the same time. Anger, rage, confusion, sadness, and betrayal rushed to my soul. They almost overwhelmed me. But I took that nuclear emotional mix and pushed it right into my soul's closet. Even after I shared my story, I never really dealt with the trauma.

People know how to give sympathy for the act of abuse or violation. But they don't consider that most of us have to stay in the vicinity of our abusers. In one way or another, we are regularly reminded by the smell of their breath, their body odor, their laugh. We often despise their freedom to laugh or their ability to live normal lives while we scream inside.

Before the song, I never talked about my sexual violation with any detail. Thirty years after the incident, when the song came out, I was applauded. But again, it wasn't for me. It was liberating for my audience. When I spoke about my own pain, the #MeToo and #TimesUp movement had not exploded onto the scene of popular culture yet. When these viral movements entered the public sphere, I looked at the uncovering of powerful people's sexual abuse and felt a sense of connection. I couldn't identify with the pain women feel in our misogynistic culture. I couldn't identify with the daily calculations they are forced to make in a society that routinely disregards their personhood (a culture men regularly participate in). But I could identify with the circumstances surrounding my abuse. I was a child. I didn't know any better. I didn't know what to do.

The sexual abuse was enough to create ripple effects of brokenness that I am still working to overcome. I also had to confront the pain of my physical abuse.

I knew instinctively that I should run. With every step my heart raced faster. I knew this wasn't a normal chase. I had mouthed off to my mother's boyfriend again. And he was over it. Children know when adults are over it, when circumstances have pushed their tolerance limits. As I ran, I knew I was in trouble. I'm not sure how I ended up on the floor. Maybe I tripped down the stairs. Maybe in a fit of rage he pushed me down. But the wind was knocked out of me long before my back met the carpet. And then he was on top of me. His punches were relentless, an avalanche of fury. I couldn't believe it was happening. "Mom . . . *Mom, help!*" My thoughts—*I'm going to die right here*—transitioned into desperate screams.

My mother's soft touch felt like sandpaper when she rubbed my scars. "I'm so sorry, baby." I whimpered as her hands massaged my bruised face. I wanted to cry out, to let out a scream. I felt like my rights had been violated. *Does anyone really care? This isn't fair!*

In light of this, I always perk up when my kids tell me, "This isn't fair!" I want to process that with them because, while I know that life isn't fair, I don't want them ever to feel like I did at their ages. Like they have no rights, no voice to appeal to those in power. That's how every adult articulated their authority. "What rights do you got, huh? You pay bills around here? You're just a kid. Shut your mouth!" In many ways, I saw Black parents mirror the message America spat to them. "Do you pay taxes? Are you a healthy contributor to society? Are you incarcerated? What rights do you have?" The trauma of systemic racism reached down through history to bring trauma to my door.

That wasn't the only physical abuse incident I experienced. Tempers would flare. Windows would break. Bodies would hit the floor. More than once I gripped the handle of the knife that sat under my bed and stared at the door, waiting for hell to burst into my room.

After my mother's boyfriend beat me, my mom separated from him for nearly a year. And in that time I was excited for it to be just us. In a weird way, there was safety in our isolation. But then he showed up with a video game system and some weak words of apology. My mom asked me if he could come back. What was I supposed to say to that? I was a kid. A ten-year-old shouldn't make that call. Even if I didn't want it, I wanted her to be happy. I just wanted to get out. I lived on eggshells and plotted vengeance.

I tell these stories because they are essential to understanding the personal chaos I would face as a grown man. I experienced physical, emotional, and sexual abuse all before the age of ten. I have spoken about this abuse before, but now my understanding of the effect is different. I've been in pain, trauma, chaos. Silently wrestling with myself as a Black man in America, I'm expressing myself as an act of resistance. A silent scream lurked in the back of my throat for decades. Amid all the shows, press appearances, and events, I was screaming, just not loud enough for anyone to hear me. I'm only beginning to understand the weight of all this years later. I grew up in an era when people would scoff at claims of "child abuse." Adults would say, "You want to know about child abuse? I was hit with a broomstick or an extension cord when my parents were mad at me!" There was a sense in which we were all hurting, all in need of therapy and recovery from the generational trauma passed down by our families.

I want to make it clear that I don't hold any bitterness toward the people who abused me. I didn't reach that place easily. I've felt all the emotions toward them, but at this moment, I'm free from the hate and the vitriol. I believe what Dr. Martin Luther King Jr. said: "Let no man pull you so low as to hate him." With God's grace and good therapy, I'm free from those feelings. But it doesn't mean that trauma didn't affect me.

The sexual abuse was tucked away because I didn't believe it affected me. It wasn't until I had my own kids that I realized the extent of that violation. If that happened to my son, I would be enraged. It put me in a world that I didn't have to be in, one that I couldn't prevent. But at the time, I was more upset about the physical abuse because it seemed so clearly wrong to be beaten by a grown adult. I would lash out, scream, goof off in school, ignore authority, all as a result of not being heard and seen. I responded out of trauma and never received healing. I lashed out in anger and fury because I knew it didn't matter. My goal at age eighteen was to go on a bank-robbing spree with my best friend, because what did it matter? There was no justice in the world. What else was there to do?

I've never talked about my abuse for fear of bringing shame to those individuals. I don't hold what they've done to me over their heads. I don't look at them as horrendous people. I look at them as broken people who function in their brokenness. The person who sexually abused me is incarcerated now, and I never considered that she had a problem that she needed people's help to work through. I never considered that she may have had a scar in her past that she was healing from. I don't know her history and what introduced such brokenness into her life. But I can't help but wonder who I would be sexually and relationally if the abuse had never happened.

Don't get me wrong, I haven't always felt this way. I've felt angry and bitter at my abusers at different times. I feel upset even when I think about what could have been. But my understanding of humanity is that we all make terrible decisions that hurt people, and those decisions are not outside of God's redemptive and restorative work. Anyone can be redeemed. Even people who commit despicable acts can receive grace. My frustration was because of the lack of consequences for my abusers. I felt like they got away with it, like I was left to pick up the broken pieces they had left behind.

Years later, as an adult, I started to feel . . . off. I wasn't off in the sense of needing more rest and vacation days. I wasn't off in the sense of needing to have more community. I felt a constant, annoying hum of anxiety. I felt like the world could cave in on me at any moment. And this was no time to have a breakdown. I was under pressure to complete albums, run a company, speak on behalf of the marginalized, love my family well, be a good friend. *Look at how many people are depending on you*, I would say to myself in quiet moments.

The more I ignored the hum, the more I started to feel more tangible consequences. I was drinking but not casually. I would drink a bottle of alcohol on a good night. Raiding the mini-bar was a common practice as soon as I arrived in my hotel. *What is wrong with me?* I wondered. I was numbing myself, drinking to go to sleep and drinking to get back up in the morning. I knew I had a problem, so I went to see a professional. I thought surely this would help. He listened while I waited for advice. Then he prescribed pills. Pills. I knew I wasn't supposed to pop those pills like candy, but I couldn't stop. They made me feel good. I at least had moments of clarity with them, but I couldn't shake this question: Am I *addicted*?

The book *The Body Keeps the Score* truly revolutionized the way I viewed my past and my trauma responses from my childhood. The author talks about the way we ignore and fail to process our trauma and the consequences of hiding what is lurking underneath the surface. He writes, "Traumatized people chronically feel unsafe inside their bodies: The past is alive in the form of gnawing interior discomfort. Their bodies are constantly bombarded by visceral warning signs, and, in an attempt to control these processes, they often become expert at ignoring their gut feelings and in numbing awareness of what is played out inside. They learn to hide from their selves."[4]

The emotional wounds I experienced as a kid are easily rationalized away. Well, *that was a long time ago. It doesn't bother me.* But I'm learning that my body doesn't have a timer. There's no timeline that it can place abuse into. My body doesn't have categories to handle it. That trauma happened, and now it's stored in places I can't hide from. While I'm trying to rationalize it, the heart and soul are saying, *We don't know how to deal with this.* These events now stored in me robbed me of normalcy, of coping mechanisms, of innocence. As an adult, I'm frustrated because that trauma I experienced robbed me of things, and there's a direct line of chaos to my present.

I discovered what it meant to have "little kid trauma" that is experienced with a little kid's mind. In some ways, that's God's form of protection for your mind, but it's also another form of abuse. Because after your abuse, your ten-year-old self thinks, *Why couldn't I fight back? I should've been able to get out of this. I should have stopped this.* My kid brain tells me that I should have prevented it, while my adult brain can process the trauma and the realities of it. I didn't have the processing

....
4 Kolk, *Body Keeps the Score*, 98–99.

skills and categories to know that there would be gaps in my family life, gaps in my marriage, gaps in my manhood. I didn't know what it meant to have my son run up to me and say, "Daddy!" with hope and love in his eyes. I didn't know what that felt like. I was just trying to survive.

When your house needs repairs, you call a plumber, an electrician, or some other type of specialist. When your suit has a defect, you call a tailor to fix the issue. When your life has a hole, who do you call? Who are you planning to lean on when someone you love dies or you lose a relationship that you felt would last forever?

Christians are not taught to value the specialists in the church, those people who are gifted in other disciplines outside of theology. I realized early on in my journey out of chaos that what I needed most was a therapist, not a theologian. I already understood doctrine. What I needed was someone who could interpret my life and make sense of why I was walking through chaos without hope of escaping the tunnel.

What people tend to do is create a marker to understand their story. When chaotic things happen, we need a narrative that helps us make sense of things so we can put them into context. Every night our brain is reconciling our narratives. The narrative that brought hell to me haunted me in the night. Amid all the success and achievement, all I could hear was, *This is who you are.* It would take years before I could identify it, and years until I could actually deal with it. But I began a dangerous pattern of self-destruction. It threatened my marriage, my platform, my very life. It spun me into a tailspin of chaos.

Other Christians told me to pray, to cry out to God, that he was somewhere listening. I couldn't hear him, and maybe I didn't want to. I just had these bottles, these pills, this self-sabotage, this trauma.

Shame is a liar. It haunts our minds, distracting us from being present and embracing what we have. Shame tells us, *You should be* _____. *If you were* _____, *you wouldn't be such a failure*. Shame silences our dreams and haunts our nightmares. Even our wildest fantasies can't live up to shame's standard of what we could be, who we should be.

In the middle of my own shame, I knew that God had something to say about shame, about the feeling of "not enough." I knew he had a way of addressing these feelings of worthlessness I experienced in my private moments without the applause and approval of others.

I would sit in silence and wait for God to take away all the shame. I begged him to remove these feelings of worthlessness from my heart. I guess I couldn't realize that he already had. He had already addressed my shame and handled my guilt. He had already dealt with my shortcomings. In these private moments, I would look up to the God I'd sung about, the God I'd told others was capable of taking everything away, and ask, "Why won't you take this shame away?" Eventually, in the silence, he whispered, *I already have.*

CHAPTER 2

You Look Like Your Father

We all must confront parts of our past. I realize how unsettling that can be, but until we confront our past, we will never be able to step into our future with true freedom. In the middle of my broken chaos, that freedom felt elusive. I would reach for it and grab nothing but air because I couldn't face my past.

Facing my past often meant me making general references to the things I used to struggle with or sins I used to be addicted to committing. That's probably the case for many Christians. We speak of our past generally to avoid dealing with the full weight of our pain. Still, it eventually catches up with us. Through my journey to restoration I've learned this simple truth: we can face our past willingly, or our lives will force us to face it. It's really that simple. We can choose to go down the valley of the shadow of death that is filled with our shame and trauma, or we can drown in our dysfunction. The choice is not easy, but it is painfully clear.

A massive part of my development came from dealing

with my own family of origin. As we grow older, many of us realize that we are duplicating the same patterns as our families in our rituals or the way we raise our kids. I chuckle whenever I say something to my kids that my mother would say to me. It can be funny, but it can also be devastating. Families shape our lives in ways we can't fully appreciate until we do the hard work of understanding the patterns that made us who we are. This is the uncomfortable part of seeking restoration—excavating our pasts, digging into the deep corners of our souls. As much as I desired freedom, the past was a place of pain, not just because of the abuse, but also because of wounds from my father and my family.

A few years ago, I made the difficult decision to stop regularly posting pictures of my family on social media. The decision was solely driven by the amount of vitriol I was exposed to on a daily basis. From slanderous comments to antagonism, I had to become quick with the block button. Until my family received death threats, I thought those comments were just a product of overly passionate people. I took those threats seriously enough to hide them from the hatred of others as much as I possibly could. Yet the shift away from sharing my family was also symbolic.

I used to pride myself on having a healthy family. After all the hell I grew up around, I would love to show off how put together my kids were, how functional we were as a unit. Family has always been a sore spot for me, a place of mixed results and mixed feelings. For the family members I know who are close, I deeply cherish their influence in my life. At the same time, family was the realm of my abuse and childhood trauma. I had been betrayed by my family's apathy toward pain and dysfunction. These wounds created a motivation to be the best possible husband and father I could be. They also created a sense of denial.

The past few years have taught me that I'm addicted to working my way out of my problems. I am driven by willpower, by the need to muscle myself out of my dysfunctional patterns. I thought I could overcome these issues with sheer will. After all, I'm a man. I'm a theologian, a celebrity, a guy with answers. I quickly learned that I couldn't "will" my way out of dysfunction.

Even with all this motivation to be a model husband and father to prove something to other people about myself, I couldn't seem to outrun my biological father's absence. As long as I can remember, all I wanted was to be loved and affirmed by him. Sometimes I just wanted him to be proud of me. Other times I just wanted him to save me. I guess I just wanted his presence to be the rock I could lean on. His absence created gaps and wounds that would haunt me for decades.

When I came to Jesus, I was excited to gain a new family that would fill in any gaps that I had felt in my childhood. I was greeted with a host of father figures, mentors, sisters, and brothers to walk with me in my journey. But I was left confused about how to address the family wounds of my past. Sure, even when mother and father forsake us, the Lord is there to be our parent. That's what Psalm 27:10 told me. I cognitively understood that he redeems these tests into testimonies for others to identify and connect with our lives.

But that didn't help me reconcile the open wound of my father leaving me.

Summers should be spent working on cars, going fishing, camping, or playing sports together. Instead, I was sent to the West Coast to spend a few months with my extended family. These trips were intended to build love and connection with my cousins and introduce me to new family members, while also giving my mom a break. Instead, they were a furious introduction to street life. I saw a side of my uncles that made me feel appreciative of their presence and terrified all at the same time.

"Get him, Crae! Don't be no punk!" Even in the middle of the chaos, I knew who said that. My uncle's voice could pierce a crowded stadium, and it was recognizable even above the scattered roar of the neighborhood onlookers. I was dizzy, but I could still hear him. *This dude can fight*, I thought as his knuckles rearranged my face. My opponent, some kid from the neighborhood, was unfazed by my weak attempts to stop him, and I knew I was in trouble. In my blurry scan of the crowd, I saw men clutching dollar bills, screaming instructions in fear of losing their bets. I felt like an animal, a prop for their enjoyment. But I knew this wasn't just for them. I was being trained. After all, my perception was that the men in my family were tough, and I felt weak.

My family members forced me to fight from a young age. In their minds they were saving me from being "a mama's boy." Because my dad wasn't around, they knew I was softer. The only way for me to become a man was for them to "beat the soft out of me." They were so committed to toughening my skin that I was treated like a pit bull and thrown into scuffles with other kids. They would place bets on me, and, of course, I always lost.

"Yo, what's wrong with you? You ain't built for this?" Some pep talk, huh? I got my face beat in, and then I heard about it from my uncle and his gangster friends. Whenever I was told that my father was tough or that he would never lose fights, I was filled with rage. I grew up hearing, "You look like your daddy," and "I bet your daddy wouldn't have. . . ." My reaction was often disgust. At a certain point, I let him go. I don't know if I hated him or if I was just tired of seeing other people interact with men in ways I never could. My only interaction with men, whether they were the kids at school, my gangster uncle in Cali, or my mom's boyfriend, involved some sort of destructive behavior. Every one of them seemed to challenge my manhood. But no one had helped me to find it.

I was never tough enough for any of the men in my life. I was sensitive and artistic, fascinated by the creative. I bobbed my head when the radio played a song I liked, and I dissected the intricacies because I thought music was beautiful—which, of course, meant I was soft, less of a man. My world only respected force and authority, or so I thought. When I was in the sixth grade, an older kid pulled a knife on me in the middle of an argument. I froze. My next instinct was to run away screaming, "Help! Help!" I didn't want to die in my school's hallway, and I knew I would lose that fight. I ran to the principal's office and hid, scared out of my mind.

"Don't be no punk!" "Look at him running away scared!" kids were yelling. I didn't care what anyone said. I didn't want to die.

When I told my mom and stepdad about the knife incident, they barely reacted. They ordered me to get a sock, fill it with pennies, and bust that kid's head wide open. "Why are you so soft?" I didn't have courage, and I was so ashamed.

When I had guns pulled on me, I never responded like a gangster. I never displayed mythical, movie-character courage. I always backed down or ran away. *Maybe I'm just not a man*, I thought. Gaps and false ideas of what it meant to be a man were passed down from my father and the other men in my life. These gaps only created the conditions for internal chaos, a lack of understanding.

My biological parents had a short-lived romance that produced me, a fling that they made a futile attempt to cement. They didn't know who they were, and when my mother got pregnant with me, they panicked. Marriage doesn't work as a last resort, so their union didn't last. My father was never around after that, except for a few random interactions. He came by once to take me shopping, and I felt like I was on top of the world. This was my *dad*, a superhero whom I had built up in my mind even though I didn't know him. We went to the mall, and he bought me the clothes I wanted. Then he drove me to his mom's house to meet her and his sister. Wow, it felt real. I was finally learning about myself.

"Oh, you look just like your daddy," his mom said. I

beamed a toothy grin when I heard her say that. That's when they noticed I had a loose tooth. In true Black family fashion, they tied some string to that tooth, attached the other end to a door handle, and yanked it out. Welcome to the family, I guess. But I didn't even care about how much that hurt. I kept smiling. I was finally with my dad. He didn't have to earn my respect. He was lionized by default. This felt different because I had finally met his family. "I love you, Dad!" is what I wanted to blurt out, but I didn't know this man. I'll save it for next time, I thought. But there was no "next time." I never saw that man again.

Sure, he called me once when I was twelve. He asked some questions and sounded like he was preoccupied with something else. When I asked if he would ever come back, his response stunned me. "Well, you know your mom remarried. You'll be good."

What? Don't you realize this house is chaotic? I'm struggling here! Help me! Again, that's what I wanted to say. But he hadn't shown me enough to prove that he would care. There was no evidence that he would have come to my rescue. My step-dad had once mocked me in a drunken rage, saying, "You gonna call your daddy? Your daddy had you, then left you. He doesn't care about you." I couldn't argue with his logic. Rumor had it, my father was a drug dealer anyway. What kind of superhero can't conquer his own addictions? I knew he wasn't coming to rescue me.

Fatherlessness is a cliché topic in the Black community. It typically sits atop the assessment list of intra-community problems in our families and neighborhoods. It's the favorite conservative talking point. "The real problem with the Black community is a lack of fathers," they say. Commentators and pundits rail as they share statistics about a lack of biological fathers' influence in the lives of their children. I get it. It's an important topic filled with nuances and considerations. As you can see, I've lived it.

While fatherlessness is a convenient scapegoat for Black pathology, I don't believe it is the foundation of everything that has happened in my life. I don't subscribe to the idea that the Black community suffers solely because of this reality. This idea lacks careful consideration of our narrative. Systemic dysfunction is in our communities because systemic evil has been visited upon us. Dr. Joy DeGruy describes this as "post-traumatic slave syndrome," a feeling that causes us to internalize the trauma of those who came before.[1] We must confront our past individually, and society must confront its past corporately.

Black people are not on these shores by choice. We are not present in this land because we wanted to be here. Our fathers were forcibly taken away from their native land and enslaved on plantations. Cruel slave masters forced them to breed with women they didn't love or know. Children were ripped from their fathers' embrace to be transported hundreds of miles away to other plantations, never to be seen again.

....
1   I originally heard her say this from a lecture she gave in London in 2008. See now her book *Post Traumatic Slave Syndrome: America's Legacy of Enduring Injury and Healing*, rev. ed. (Joy Degruy Publications, 2017).

This is not simply a matter of theory or academic discussion. I can track this legacy through my own family of origin. My great-great-grandmother Emilene was a slave who was brought over from West Africa when she was nine years old. She had to figure out life in another country. Jim Crow laws antagonized and terrorized our communities. Terror tactics, like lynching Black men and women, were used to discourage the broader Black community from speaking out about injustice. And while it's easy to say that circumstances have improved, Black men in low-income situations work themselves into the ground, often struggling just to provide for their families. The crack epidemic, mass incarceration, and police brutality are further indications of the need for improvement. How hypocritical it is to point a judgmental finger in the direction of the Black community when three fingers of judgment are pointed right back at the systemic evil of the status quo.

Despite all these systemic factors, I do acknowledge that my father still had the agency to love me, and he chose not to embrace me. He still could have provided a space for me to be vulnerable, and I had none. He still could have protected me from the violating hands of my abuser. He could have defended me when my stepdad pummeled me. He still could have cared. He should have cared, and he didn't. Fatherlessness forms a web of issues that I couldn't even begin to unravel in this volume, and all fatherless Black people carry this web within them, whether we acknowledge it or not. Fatherlessness is not the sole basis for problems in Black lives, but it has created personal chaos.

I'm still trying to unpack the effects of my father wounds to this day. I have worked hard to purge bitterness and hatred from my heart, but ignoring what was robbed from me isn't easy. Recovering from my father's absence has been a life-long process, a painful but necessary engagement with a dark time in my life. When, as a young Christian, I spoke about my fatherlessness, I had a tendency to skip the messier parts of my story and use only those salient details for a testimony service or to shock listeners into seeing the radical power of gospel redemption. Now it's a little more complicated than that. I see how my failure to comprehensively address my relationship with my father created even more chaos in my life.

My perspective began to shift when I began to wonder, *Did my father pass anything down to me? Do I act like him or have similar interests? Can I learn anything about my past from his reputation?* I started to see that some of my personal preferences didn't come from my mother. She is a beautiful Black mother, with the force to walk through a wall to help the people she loves. I see her as a go-getter, stubborn and intelligent. I can see all the complicated ways she passed down those traits to me. But my mother is not analytical in the same ways that I am. She does not crave intel in the same way that I voraciously read and digest information. I wonder where I get that from. Is that from my dad? My father had a reputation for loving science fiction and geek culture, something I also deeply love. Is that interest hereditary? As I grow older, I wonder about how his personality was passed on to me.

Why do I get upset when my kids don't drink all the

milk in their cereal bowls? Because that's what I grew up experiencing. Since I can now process things in light of my narrative, I can prevent creating new traumas.

Another side of me had an affinity for romanticizing street life. The men in my family place an emphasis on being tough and displaying their masculinity. They're gangsters. They're incarcerated. Especially after my conversion I had a sense that I had let them down. I was a Christian man who hadn't been in any street shootouts. I never "ascended the hill," so I figured I wasn't a real man.

Similarly, my mother once expressed how her dad's side of the family also created patterns. Some battled alcoholism. I thought, Oh, *maybe that's how I can drink for twenty days and it's not a big deal.* She told me stories of addictions, and I see it in my own life. There's a part of myself that I still don't know. A part that makes me think, *What kind of man would I be if I actually knew my dad?*

"Ayo!" The neighborhood OG's voice cut through street-corner clowning and stopped us in our tracks. "These Crips keep comin' 'round here. . . . Y'all gotta get some getback. Y'all got a gun?" One of my friends swallowed hard and nodded to a tree where he hid our lone weapon of defense from rival gangs. "Cool. The next time they come around here, you *shoot first.*"

I spent summers with my uncle, getting tough, running the streets, and searching for significance. I enjoyed my time there, even though it was filled with chaos. I now know that's all they knew. I saw shootings, drug arrests, and other things a kid shouldn't be exposed to at that age. But I'll never forget when that guy told us to "shoot first." I looked around like I was in a dream. My friends' eyes were glued to him, drinking in his instructions and processing how they would act on them. *What is wrong with y'all?* I thought to myself as I half listened to advice that I just knew would get one of us killed. This was my moment of clarity. Forget this "tough guy" act. I don't have to live like this. At that moment, before my conversion to Christ, before I had the privilege of healthy community, I knew I had options. Earlier that year my auntie had sent me a postcard from Japan. I stared at the scenery for the longest time. It helped me to see that the world is bigger than this neighborhood pettiness. I didn't want to be a street dude, and I wasn't built for it.

I had to fill the gaps in with something. I had to find some outlet to prove myself to others, something that would help me make sense of my existence. I couldn't identify with these tough men in my family, but hip-hop was a place of affirmation and acceptance for me. Someone was recognizing me for the gift that I was.

When I found hip-hop, I felt like it was all I needed to fill in any of my life gaps. I didn't want to excavate the problems of my past to get healed. I didn't want to enter into the chaos because I was convinced it would consume me.

When I stepped onto the stage for the talent show at the Boys & Girls Club at age eleven, I never expected any of my hood friends to love what I did. But watching their frenzied reaction made me say, "Oh, I love this." I enjoyed hip-hop music as a consumer, but to be appreciated for performing was a different level. It felt right. After I ran from the knife-wielding kid in the sixth grade, I had my moment of redemption. I beat a notorious tough kid in a rap battle. That was the first moment that felt special. He was perceived as a young gangster, a tough guy just like the men in my life. I wasn't quite sure how people perceived me, but I knew it wasn't positive. They thought I was scared, cowardly, or unathletic. In any case, I felt like I didn't belong. I would lash out, but not in the same way as other kids. I already felt ashamed because I had had a knife pulled on me.

When I beat that kid in that rap battle, something shifted in my heart.

Slithering like a snake in the grass
Taking you and your crew you gotta know is an easy task.
When I strike it'll hurt like a snakebite.
You gotta know I make you wet your pants
when your mama tucks you in at night.
I'm scary, so very the lunatic psycho
Guilty but you don't see me running from the po-po.
Been in twenty-one fights this year, month week
day, I don't play stop until the 9 spray.

"Ohhhhhh." The crowd erupted. I was engulfed by the same people who made fun of me. I hadn't even hit puberty yet. My voice hadn't changed. But my consumption of hip-hop culture paid off in the admiration of my friends. Maybe

I couldn't beat anyone up, but I could beat them with my words. I won, and it kept going. I was the reigning rap champion. No one could touch me. Rap became part of the identity of my reputation. "Y'all know Lecrae can rap." That was the identity marker I needed to ignore all this manhood chaos that I couldn't escape.

Even after my conversion, I still clung to this part of my identity. It looked a little different at that point because people weren't just praising my skill. They praised how my skill showcased my devotion to Jesus. The crowds surrounded me, just enough to hide the chaos. I was addicted to alcohol and popping pills to numb myself from the pain of addressing my past. I came perilously close to sabotaging the beautiful family God gave me. The pressure to prove my manhood shifted into a pressure to prove that my devotion to God was legitimate. The bloggers, the theologians, the fans were watching like hawks to see if I would slip up. And the culture considered me a standard-bearer for this different wave of music. They were tempting me with what they passed at parties and private events.

In the middle of navigating this broken reality, I was forced to ask, *Where is the script to show me what it means to be a man? Who will show me what it means to be a father? If my own father failed, how can I succeed? If my own dad was a screw-up, I guess I'm destined to be that as well, right? Where's my pathway to fulfill this role?*

I remember reading the work of a professor who specializes in the divinity of Jesus. He remarked that in the Torah there are detailed scripts of what the temple priests were supposed to do. With painful attention to detail, each of the priests had to follow the temple rules. Those who ignored or broke the rules received strict, even fatal, consequences. Their role as priest was emphasized rather than the person. They were seen through the standard of their position in the nation. Most of us can't name many priests from the Old Testament, but almost all of us can name at least a few of the kings.

But ironically, there are no specific rules in Scripture for being a king. Sure, there are Proverbs that they could cling to and general principles that would be wise for kings. But often they would succumb to the temptations of lust, conquest, and power-based evils. There was no script for how to rule, no script for how to lead, no script for royalty. This gave me hope because, as a man, I don't necessarily have a script for how to exist in my world. I couldn't follow the script that came from the men around me or from my father. But over time I have become convinced that God had a script for me to follow. His script is simply to love him completely, love my neighbors faithfully, and navigate life in light of these two commands. My responsibility is to love my wife and kids well and remain faithful to them. That's what it means to be a father even when I don't have a father. For years I was convinced there was a "man script" for every contour of my behavior, and God had to show me there are all types of men in his kingdom, living different but faithful lives. There is no complicated script. My liberty is in simplicity. Love God and love others well. That's it.

What holds us back from addressing our families of

origin? I'm convinced that a large part of what holds us back is our fear. Fear makes us shrink back in a false version of ourselves. Fear keeps us from engaging in necessary conversations and confronting our unhealthy habits. Fear binds us to *What will others think if I admit this?* Fear makes us ashamed of who God created us to be.

I sat across from my father recently. It was the first conversation we'd had in decades. I looked into his eyes, examined what was in his soul, and felt his pain. I did look like my father, but I was no longer trapped as he was. The man who wasn't present for most of my childhood was imprisoned by his own fears, bound by his own mistakes. He was plagued with addictions he couldn't beat, expectations he couldn't fulfill. In that moment, I felt overwhelming sorrow for the hatred I had directed at him for so many years. I am still working through the pain, still battling with the wounds I felt, but at least I now have a perspective from which to approach them.

CHAPTER 3

Church Hurt Is the Worst

We aren't surprised by how dysfunctional our families are. We aren't shocked that we are the product of the sometimes chaotic choices our parents or relatives made. Their patterns can easily become ours and have the power to shape our future. But few of us are prepared for church dysfunction. I was unprepared for what chaotic behavior would look like from fellow Christians. Most people, when they come to Jesus, are so enthusiastic about their transformation that they are blind to the flaws hidden in plain sight of other believers around them. That was my experience as well. I was so overjoyed to have a family I could identify with that I ignored the brokenness. Truth be told, I should have known better.

As someone once said, "Church hurt is the worst hurt." Church hurt comes in the form of betrayal, backbiting, marginalization, embarrassment, shame, and even abuse. Church hurt can be seen in the eyes of the person who believed the church was serious about their invitation "Come as you are."

Everyone has experienced a measure of pain from attending church because that's the nature of interacting with others. But some of us have faced the church's disdain and condemnation. Some churches aren't just flawed; they're toxic.

I've watched closely over the last few years as believers have called out churches for various levels of hypocrisy. Brave women have brought attention to the heinous cycles of sexual assault for other women and even children. Women like Rachael Denhollander, Trillia Newbell, Dr. Christina Edmondson, and many others have stood in the light and called out the darkness they see in our treatment of the vulnerable.

Jemar Tisby talks about the racial toxicity of the American church in his book *The Color of Compromise.*[1] He addresses these issues by documenting the compromise of the church with racism from the founding days of this country until now. Since churches were instituted in the American context, Christians haven't always lived up to the call of Christ. From the genocide of Native peoples to the promotion of slavery to Jim Crow and other forms of oppression, the church doesn't always represent Jesus well. I've realized that depending on what tribe we have committed to, we may or may not be familiar with these historical events and the theology that created them. I'm learning that much of our understanding of God is shaped by whose version of Christianity we find most appealing. Most of us interact with church through our own experiences.

....

1   Jemar Tisby, *The Color of Compromise: The Truth about the American Church's Complicity in Racism* (Grand Rapids: Zondervan, 2019).

Just as I had to understand my childhood and family trauma through my personal history, I had to understand my present experiences through my history with organized religion. My relationship with church has always influenced my life, even if it looked much different in different seasons of my life. As with many Black Americans, the traditional Black church runs deep in my bloodline. My great-grandfather, known as Bishop Bryant to his congregation, was a Church of God in Christ minister who was apparently a fiery preacher. My uncle, along with others on my mother's side of the family, were also preachers.

Writer Kiese Laymon references this dynamic in his memoir *Heavy*: for most of us, the version of the faith we grew up in was nurtured by our grandmothers, our mothers, our aunts, and other women in our lives.[2] Black women always make up the backbone of the Black church. The only grandmother I knew was a deeply committed believer. After living the first forty years of her life for herself, my grandmother became what the old folks call a "souled out" believer in Christ.

Through my grandmother's example, I was introduced to a serious walk with the Lord, what theologians today refer to as a "missional" life. She lived her faith out loud in everything she did. Grandma would take me with her on the Southeast San Diego streets as she passed out bread and other food to the homeless population. We even went to Mexico to visit orphanages and care for those the Bible calls

....

2 Kiese Laymon, *Heavy: An American Memoir* (New York: Scribner, 2018).

"the least of these." I vividly remember watching her patio preaching every Monday night with other Black women. The services were far from formal. Those women just loved God and did everything they could to cultivate a closer relationship with him.

In contrast, I never found the organized institution of church appealing. I didn't understand why people would dress up in fancy clothes every week just to go to the church and pretend they weren't messed up. I saw the emotion and couldn't connect to the passion. I heard the sermons, and most of them went over my head. When I was a kid, we would attend services only on Christmas and Easter, and even then I struggled to stay awake and pay attention. After experiencing the love and care I saw my grandma give others around her who were less fortunate, traditional church had little appeal.

College drastically changed my perception of what church and faith could be for me. I was attracted to ministries that didn't have the trappings of organized religious institutions. When freshly converted college students get together, the result is typically an explosion of energy. I found that in college campus ministries like The Impact Movement. I enjoyed this movement because it didn't resemble traditional religious practices. I felt something fresh, something vibrant; and it made me even more curious about a relationship with Jesus.

After my initial encounter with Jesus after college, I attended a local COGIC church in my area. I look back on that time differently now than when I was regularly attending the services. I remember feeling the whiplash of my early experiences with traditional church. I didn't understand much of what was happening in their services. I would ask myself questions about the way they worshiped, their passion, their fervor. The rituals weren't appealing to me, but I loved Jesus, so I was committed to it. Part of me was trying to study the church culture to find out where I fit in. What was this expression of my Blackness and my faith? Did my faith have anything to say to my culture?

As a new convert, I was awkwardly navigating what it meant to worship in a Black church setting. *How should I lift my hands? What should I do when the pastor is preaching? Am I doing this right?* They clapped, praised, and interacted far differently from my college Bible study group. I felt like they loved each other well, but I was so unfamiliar with the customs that I didn't know if I fit in. Many people I've talked to have expressed their awkwardness as they came to God and tried to interact with a church tradition they did not understand.

I would interact with many more expressions of Christianity. I even visited a local charismatic megachurch from time to time. I remember listening to the pastor's vignettes and being completely confused. I didn't realize that I had been saved not just into Christianity but into a conservative expression of the faith. This version of faith made me dislike overly emotional expressions of following Christ. I knew I loved Jesus and urban culture, but I needed something to intellectually stimulate me. As I studied the Bible more, I realized that I couldn't identify with the televangelist version of the faith. I saw pastors praying over obscure objects and saying they possessed "anointing." That seemed more like mysticism than faithful Christian practice. And what I learned in Bible studies seemed to be in conflict with the COGIC church.

A year into my faith, I developed a deep disdain for the Black church. I didn't realize it until much later, but I homogenized the Black church experience. I assumed all Black churches were exactly like the ones I had previously attended. Those churches had seemed to be dominated by preachers and personalities obsessed with prosperity and profit who used the congregation for their own personal benefit. I couldn't see their commitment to biblical theology. I had been indoctrinated into a specific brand of Christianity and assumed that these churches would mirror that expression if they were truly following Jesus.

I was blinded by my own arrogance and ignorance of Black church practices. I didn't know about ring shouts or hush arbors. I didn't associate the phrases they repeated with a fully formed doctrine of love that came from treating others like they would want to be treated. I read Dr. King for his political speeches but not for his sermons and theology. I missed how the theological foundations of Black pastors built the foundation for the politics and activism that produced change. I completely missed the theological rootedness of the Black church. I was addicted to being intellectually "right."

Eventually the tribe I found myself attracted to was obsessed with theological accuracy, so eventually many of my Black Christian friends and I left the predominately Black

Christian spaces in favor of places that were "more solid," another word we often use to describe white conservative Christian spaces. The leader of our college Bible study group was mentored by a white theologian, and eventually we ended up in a white church. The experience was even more different from the places that we were accustomed to being in. The emotion, passion, and expression of Black church spaces were completely absent. The lights were much lower, and the preaching was monotone. The preacher would quote white men who had long been dead, conservative thinkers who spoke in lofty prose. Who were these guys?

This new brand of theology I was being introduced to was called "Reformed theology." Reformed theology, or "Calvinism," is a belief system built on the idea that God is above all things, and that we are lost without him. These beliefs appealed to my intellect but in a cold, disconnected way. I began drinking from the fountain of Reformed theologians' wisdom, believing that I was becoming smarter than everyone else. Their theology was far more Father, Son, and Holy Bible in its emphasis. I would rarely hear about anything emotional from these sources, just strong intellectual theology. I devoured books from John Piper, J. I. Packer, and John MacArthur, among others. Their books and sermons pointed me back to an even deeper tradition of European thinkers, such as John Calvin, John Owen, and the Puritans.

It's hard to describe just how much this theological system consumed me. I was overrun with knowledge and obsessed with "right doctrine." What amazed me was that I couldn't "turn it off." It didn't matter if the preacher was on television, was in my church, or was even someone I knew, the overarching question I would ask was the same: "Is this biblical?" I felt a sense of empowerment because I had understanding that I previously was unaware even existed, and I wanted to show off just how much I knew. I wanted to let them know I was one of the "good ones," not like those foolish preachers who looked just like me. This desire led me to look for error everywhere, questioning, *Who is solid? Who is biblical?* Self-righteousness fed into my insecurity.

My spiritual journey was thrown into hyperdrive when I started incorporating this theology into my music. I would spend hours trying to weave in big theological concepts over the southern musical sounds, because I needed to infiltrate my community with sound doctrine and good theology, not that foolish Black church stuff they were receiving every weekend.

> But even if you don't know systematic theology
>
> Or eschatology
>
> You know Jesus is who you wanna to seek.[3]

> And when sin in looks like the pressure,
>
> I'm havin to turn quick.
>
> A sin sick, so merk it like John Owen.
>
> You know when Jesus the Christ you
>
> can pay him but still owe him.[4]

....

3 Lyrics from "Souled Out," from the album *Real Talk* (Reach, 2004; Cross Movement Records, 2005).

4 Lyrics from "Unashamed," featuring Tedashii, from the album *After the Music Stops* (Cross Movement Records and Reach, 2006).

The voices I respected fell in love with the creativity of using their study in this novel way. They were captivated by me taking their concepts and using them to create catchy hooks to be shouted by mixed-race audiences. My lyrics were almost like a cheat code for Reformed theology.

So, the theology of the lyrics wasn't an issue, but my motivation for using them was. Inwardly, I was being consumed with the desperate desire to be affirmed by other men. At this point it didn't matter if they were white or Black; I just needed someone to affirm how special I was. I needed to be the unicorn, the one who would be valued above the others in my culture. I remember writing a line in the album *Real Talk* just so that listeners would catch the clues of me being a trusted source of theology. After all, it was all about being solid and biblical.

Without a father in my life, I was pleased to be affirmed by any man, whichever one would applaud me the loudest. I thought this was what I needed in my life: real father figures. My desire to be loved and affirmed led me to use my gifts to advance other peoples' agendas. I was performing for other people, and though some may have genuinely loved me, for others, the oddity of a rapper spouting weighty theology was a minstrel show. As my platform grew and the affirmation swelled, I leaned harder into the persona. I recorded interviews on popular Christian outlets, minimizing the effect of white Christian hypocrisy. I downplayed that at least some of these Reformation-era theologians whom my tribe regularly affirmed were slaveholders. I had to. I was the safe, secret obsession for white suburban Christian kids.

For years I performed and spoke at a sports camp in Missouri. While I was there, the white counselors would treat me like I was a precious jewel. I lapped up their attention because they saw me not just as an artist but as a trusted source of theology. Most of these camps were attended by white suburban kids who loved every second of my music and my theological presentation. I remember thinking, *Why would I ever accept bookings in Black churches again?* After all, the white churches would book me on time and pay me better than my own people. In Black churches I was an afterthought, mostly relegated to an experiment by a risky, edgy youth pastor who was trying to modernize his church community. But the white pastors would memorize my songs and use them in sermon illustrations or announcement videos. They really embraced me, or so I thought.

My life changed when some of the white heroes whose works I'd read were now publicly embracing and affirming my artistry. For a kid who desperately wanted attention and love from his family and friends, this was like jet fuel. It was all the significance I had ever wanted. I let my guard all the way down with this group of people. I was the slave who had been accepted into the master's house.

It was as if these people invited me in to play for dinner or make a couple comments at the family meeting. I became the person who would interpret Blackness for them so they could "reach" my community. They weren't looking to glean from the perspective of Black thinkers, the Black community, or even the Black church. They just wanted me to be an echo chamber for their point of view. To take it a step further, they wanted me to act as a correcting agent for my people. I was sent to rebuke the "slaves in the field" or the streets or the ghetto, and to admonish the prosperity preachers.

I was so consumed with having the approval of these white theologians that it never occurred to me that their acceptance was temporal, that they only loved my opinions but not my essence. I was being waved around as evidence that God could redeem from the inferior Black Christian community and truly transform even a hip-hop artist. Some of these people knew what they were doing. For them, this was a time-tested technique of cultural colonizing. Others just had the privilege of not being forced to think about the ramifications of their actions. They had the privilege of erasing my culture and using my skin. They had the luxury of the status quo of theology and culture.

This is the problem with much of American Christian culture. Instead of interrogating and confronting the motives that exist behind their cultural expression of following Jesus, many Christians are content with keeping the power dynamics as they are, unwilling to address their own complicity in creating hierarchy where none should be.

At the time, evangelicalism wasn't even a conversation. I had no clue about the political or cultural connections that led to white Christian identification with certain social positions. I had just met Jesus, so whatever these men said was absolute truth to me. I was consumed with self-hate and even hated my culture.

These white men didn't love Lecrae. They didn't love the complicated parts of me, the parts that were still in flux.

They loved the assured Lecrae, the one who had it all figured out. The one who would resurrect hip-hop—without the filth—for God's glory and their children's safe entertainment. It wasn't about me at all. They loved what I could do for them. Most Americans tend to believe that they are "a-cultural." They tend to think they don't have any sort of cultural bias or skewed views that are directly influenced by the world they create. Most Americans view themselves as "the winners" of the narrative of the world, so how could anyone else's perspective be right and their perspective be wrong?

Most of us don't realize how we import and export culture. We call the expressions of someone's heritage by its moniker. We do this in food, music, fashion, and even beauty products. It's called Japanese food, or Mexican food. Why? Because our food (American food) is regular food. Our music is "popular music." We look at American culture as "normal" and everything else is strange or foreign. Sadly, most people who believe they are appreciating a person of color and their culture are actually appropriating them.

In all this journey, I adopted the self-assurance of these white theologians. I never thought for a second that we could be wrong. After all, who else had this complex system of theology? How could anyone argue with any sort of authority? I was fully "sunk," to use a popular analogy. White was bigger, and bigger was better. I was increasingly disenchanted with my people for not being present on the same platforms that I was on. Man, *where are we*? I would think to myself at every event, conference, or performance. I wanted to make sure "solid" Black voices were given the shine that I was receiving.

Surely it wasn't just me who was receiving appreciation from this majority culture.

I remember intentionally choosing more tours that were in Black spaces, colleges, and Black church conferences. Thinking I would convince them they wre missing out on this wonderful theology I had to offer, it led to far more frustration with them. I performed at a prominent megachurch conference and was sick with internal conflict. I was energized by the love of the participants but frustrated by how tightly they clung to their culture. Why did they have to wear suits and listen to gospel music? There were so many other better options. I thought I was giving them a gourmet meal while they were settling for "fast food."

Despite all this acceptance and love from white Christians, I felt a sneaking tinge of suspicion creep up in my heart. This was likely a function of my personality, which rejects being used as a prop for anything. The countercultural nature of my heritage started to suspect that I was being used for my platform instead of my personhood. Even though I felt affirmed, I held back parts of myself that I imagined white Christians wouldn't fully embrace. I put away the urban culture I loved. I figured they weren't ready to see those parts of my expression.

Then the Christian worldview started to infringe on my culture. Not the biblical elements of the gospel but the cultural elements of American Christianity started to sour on me when I stepped into more mainstream settings. The Christian worldview is built on a strict sacred-secular divide. On one side is redeemed music that is explicitly Christian in all its content. On the other side is evil secular music that corrupts the souls of those who listen to it. The two are declared to be polar opposites, but I never understood the distinction. God can speak through any artist or creative, right? I began to see people in the Bible who were "secular" but still used mightily by God in their spheres of influence. I began to think that I could be used to reach all hip-hop, not just the Christian subculture that I was comfortable with.

As I subtly pushed the artificial boundaries of the sacred-secular debate, the legalistic wing of Reformed Christianity started to turn on me. I was attracted to the systematic qualities of the doctrine they preached, but I started to see how they also established rigid categories for how art should be interpreted and created. I realized that if I didn't make the kind of music they deemed to be explicitly Christian, their embrace would loosen. As my art expanded, my theology began to broaden. I listened to different traditions that valued how excellent the music is, not just how explicitly Christian its presentation is.

My *Church Clothes* project was the first time I shifted away from performing music considered strictly Christian, and acceptance of my music by my former audience quickly diminished. From that point on, I wasn't trying to be the old Lecrae who incorporated the Puritans into every song. I wanted to be the artist whom a young Black man could identify with in his situation, whatever it was. I was slowly pressing out of the religious box I had been given, creating space for my music to reflect all of me, not just my theological understanding. As I anticipated, my heroes did not follow me. Initially they were curious about my shift, but when it became clear I would not be as safe an option for their followers, I was greeted with radio silence.

My desire was that hip-hop would see a different side of following Jesus, one that firmly maintained biblical convictions while also refusing to discard people on their journey with God. My tribe didn't see it that way. They were fixated on my collaborations with mainstream artists. They could not believe that I was appearing on the same song as someone who would talk about street life on their own projects. I remember doing a song from the album *Gravity* with Big K.R.I.T., and the backlash was relentless. I was scrolling through social media comments and blurted out, "Wow, they're tribal." I began to see it wasn't just "them"; I had also become tribal.

My public interviews were analyzed with a fine-tooth comb to see if I was departing from the faith. Every BET interview or awards-show acceptance speech was expected to include a Scripture reference or an explicit claim to faith, or it was a sign of my compromise. Public appearances became joyless from anticipating the pushback of a tribal people ready to see my fall. I thought they loved me. Why were they so hard on me?

I began to see subtle double standards in the music business. It would be okay for a CCM artist to post a picture with a country music star, or even appear alongside them at an event. But sharing a video with hip-hop artists or incorporating them in my music was a cardinal sin. It felt like it was only "secular" when there was a Black artist involved.

At the same time as I encountered the shift, I was expanding my views on race and politics (more on that later). I discovered parts of church history that disturbed me. Weren't these the church fathers I was taught to idolize? Why were they treating my people like this? Why didn't my tribe tell me about their participation in these sins of racism and slavery? I felt betrayed, like the truth was hidden from me. I was slowly becoming disillusioned by a group of believers who were so sure of themselves. They were convinced that they had cornered the market on truth.

Then I started to see how "Christian" the entertainment side of the church actually was. I went on tours and saw substance abuse, womanizing, and other things most people would never expect. I was shocked to see what was acceptable even in greenrooms. So many were drinking and participating in debauchery to their heart's content. To be clear, I was struggling with my own brokenness, so my response was not filled with judgment, just surprise at the facade.

One of my first popular songs was "Take Me as I Am," a plea for God to take all of me, even the broken, dirty parts of my story. I realized at this point of my journey that I was exhausted from living as the representative of a group that didn't really accept me for who I am.

At this point of my chaotic journey, I was attempting to work through my own brokenness. I was addicted and self-medicating. I was haunted by my past and ashamed of my mistakes. And the very thing I needed, a community of believers, was the very group that I thought was rejecting me. Just at the time when I most needed private support, I encountered public ridicule.

Around this time, I remember our house had a leak that was impossible to stop. I tried everything and couldn't find the exact position of the leak, even though it was creating a puddle in a part of my house. I called all the experts, expecting them to give me a quick fix. After many calls and an estimate, I received grim news: the only way to find the leak was to expose the wall, identify the leak, and rebuild the wall. This turned what I thought would be a minor job into a reconstruction project. Without this vital work, the leak would continue and slowly erode the strength of the wall.

Just as deconstruction was needed to repair the wall, deconstruction of my faith to ground zero was what I needed to reestablish my faith. Without understanding everything that I needed to do, I knew I would be forced to ask some hard questions about the theology I was claiming as my own. I knew I would have to address all my biases. I would have to address my denominational bias. I realized I would have to confront the biases I possessed from seeing through an American lens, or a male-dominated lens, or all the subtle biases that slowly created a puddle of self-righteousness and tribalism. I needed to deconstruct them all.

As I began to reconstruct my theology, I realized that I hadn't read broadly enough. I realized that my circle of influence or frame of reference had been far too constricting and limiting. Most painfully, I realized that I despised the contributions of the Black church. Just because I was taught to think with my mind and not feel with my body, I was disconnected from my people and from the very theology that rejected the narrow tendencies of Western Christianity. The same theology that gave Black slaves hope in the cotton fields continues to strengthen us today in times of oppression and injustice. The God of the oppressed became real to me.

In most cases, the root of our problem as Christians is addiction to religion. Christianity is a faith with a set of beliefs that includes rituals and rules. The problem is not our set of beliefs, rituals, or rules. The problem is the cultural practices we've baptized in biblical language. So much of my life has been spent meeting the cultural expectations of other Christians based on minor biblical teachings rather than on the major commands of loving God and others. This type of devotion was displayed by the Pharisees who opposed Jesus, who wanted to parade around and show everyone else how good they were by the rules they kept. I came to this painful realization: I wasn't devoted to God. I was devoted to my devotion to God.

All my works and self-righteousness became badges I wore to parade how right I was for others. I wanted to appear good instead of being good. I wanted to be seen as wise and faithful to others, especially the gatekeepers of theology. For all my years of discipleship and theological training, I couldn't outrun my own motives.

I saw that my faith had become so Western that I wasn't looking at global voices for contribution and instruction. What do my Ethiopian sisters and brothers have to say to our Americanized, privileged gospel? What do my Colombian sisters and brothers have to teach us that we have refused to incorporate in our books? What do Black women have to say to our male-dominated gospel that erases their immense contributions to the kingdom of God? I was convicted that I had ignored entire elements of God's kingdom for just one area of emphasis.

I began to put these diverse perspectives in conversation with one another and to interrogate my own perspectives in light of their input. I knew I couldn't leave Jesus behind. Despite the failure of his church, I couldn't abandon how real he was to me. Other scenarios later in my journey caused me to question him, but I would always run back like the son in Jesus's parable whose father was ready to embrace him. I determined to keep Jesus at the center and rebuild.

I am no longer willing to accept Christian expression that refuses to hear voices from the margins. Christ's body is global and diverse. The perspectives that come from the people who make up Christ's body reveal the brilliance of our Creator, like the different facets of a diamond. Erasing the edges is equal to denying the beauty of God. Others have different contexts and areas of emphasis, but they should be heard and valued as legitimate.

Rather than being self-assured of how right my theology is, I can now freely admit that I don't have everything figured out yet. I know that my theology is a work in progress and will be complicated by life circumstances and other perspectives. What I can say is that the family of God is far more global, diverse, and eclectic than we're comfortable admitting. It will challenge all our notions of who deserves God's grace and who has a right to describe God's work.

PART 2

RECKONING WITH THE CHAOS AROUND ME

CHAPTER 4

How Many More Lives
Have to Be Taken?

Black lives matter! Black lives matter! No justice, no peace!" The atmosphere was charged with anguish and frustration. I originally planned to stand on the outskirts of the protest march, just to observe, to fade to the background of the demonstration. But the crowd was a living organism, drawing me in. Their pull was magnetic. I couldn't just watch. I had to join them. I wanted to join them. These protesters were angry, and understandably so. Yet another hashtag had filled our social media pages. Another Black body was lying dead in the streets, with little hope for justice.

I debated going to the rally and planned to stand out of the line of sight just in case people would see my face or recognize me. I never intended to be a distraction to their demonstration, but just like them, I was in pain. This feeling wasn't just disappointment; it was a feeling I hadn't felt before. Well, not since the police pulled me over years earlier.

Not since the last time I was profiled. The more I heard; the more I was drawn into the crowd's fierce anger. The crowd's energy was almost chaotic. Mass trauma had overwhelmed all of us. The rhythmic chants hit the air louder with each word. We were exhausted from death, tired of the videos, fed up by injustice.

Every week my group chat text threads were on fire. I held a few friends close to my chest throughout the years, and all of us felt the same sense of pain, only to different degrees. My friends were crying out on social media to no avail. After all, our followers wanted our theology, our rhymes, our concert experiences, but not our Blackness. They didn't want *us*, not all of us. We were feeling unheard in the noise of the media cycle. Without a way to use my social media presence for anything productive, I needed to find another way. I had to do something. So I went to the rally.

I was unprepared for the level of energy. But their energy was understandable. Who was I to stop them? I remember watching how the movie *Selma* highlighted the tactical organization of the civil rights movement. Dr. King, Malcolm X, John Lewis, Diane Nash, and so many others strategically applied pressure when the cameras were on and reporters were present. They baited the police officers into pulling out their most violent discrimination so the American public could witness their brutality. They had a plan, a strategy to advance the movement.

Those who attended this protest didn't seem interested in any talk of strategy. Their infectious chants led to marching, and without a clear direction, the crowd began to act out of their collective trauma. People in the crowd threw bottles, broke store windows, and smashed police cars. They grabbed whatever they could and hurled it at whatever was valuable. My pain turned into shock as I saw the protest slip into something more dangerous. My instincts were to say something and do something immediately. "Stop! We don't have to do this! This isn't the way!" I tried to talk them out of it, but I couldn't stand in the way of their outrage. Their cries had gone unheard for so long that they were speaking in the only language they could speak: riot.

Sometimes I think about that night and how I was so sure I had to do something, but for years I had been unsure about challenging the racism of the theologians I admired. Why was that? That night some rioted, and others marched peacefully with children in tow. Others just cried and screamed. But I couldn't help asking, "Who is leading this demonstration? What are the goals? What will be accomplished when we leave?" I had felt that confusion for some time.

Like most Black Americans, I don't know much about my family's history. Most Black families avoid sharing intimate details of our lineage for many reasons. We don't have the privilege of tracing my family's ancestors back to a specific country or region with any certainty. But I know enough to be enraged. I know enough to be upset. Unlike most Black Americans, the early parts of my life were spent in Black-dominant spaces. In that way my childhood was unique. I was used to being in the majority during elementary school, especially when I visited my extended family in southeast San Diego.

The age-old question for many socially conscious peers is "When did you first realize you were Black?" When did the difference shake you into reality? My earliest memory of even recognizing ethnic distinction was when a family member jokingly told me I was "dancing like a white boy." Huh? My young mind didn't register the distinction because I couldn't remember ever seeing a white kid dance. What do *they* dance like? I started paying attention to television and my childhood friends to see if there really was a difference. Processing any form of cultural difference that early in life was hard.

But differences started becoming clearer when I asked to visit my friend's house to hang out. I was startled when he said no. I thought we were friends, or at least close to becoming real friends. I was surprised but not too hurt, until his sister told me the real reason. "My mom doesn't want you to come over to our house because you're Black." Huh? I was disturbed and confused. So, *maybe this is a serious issue*, I thought. I started to detect differences more easily. I saw how certain kids treated me. I watched how the standard was different for kids in my class. Some differences were obvious. I knew that this white kid was wrong when he called me a "nigger," but I punched him in the face and knocked his tooth out because my mom said, "Don't you let nobody call you that." It didn't matter that I was in first grade. He had to pay for that.

This dynamic of observing lasted for years. I saw more and more, but I was still in the majority setting in that context until I moved to Denver. That was culture shock for me.

Even in the Blackest parts of the city, there was no avoiding the presence of white people. Attending Martin Luther King Middle School didn't even shield me from their presence. Those kids were everywhere. They were the majority in every area of life.

As I progressed through middle school, the lines became more clearly drawn. Our interests became more segregated. I loved urban culture. Hip-hop, graffiti, stylish overalls, and sneakers—all of these were native to my expression. I gravitated naturally toward these things and the people who also liked them. The Black kids started to hang with one another at lunch, and the other ethnic groups naturally huddled together. We started slowly siphoning off from the broader melting pot.

High school was a different experience. My school was completely Black. I instinctively floated back into my default cultural expression. In my spare time, I would stay in the hood markets and swap meets where I bought mix CDs and fake Tommy Hilfiger shirts. These were the places I loved to be. These were the places I could truly be myself.

I spent my last two years of high school in the Dallas area. When we moved there, my mother viewed this as our chance to have what we needed. Giving me an opportunity at a great education was everything for her.

We found a community called Duncanville that was affordable but also very Black. Their education quality wasn't high, and when my mother saw that the best schools were in a North Dallas community, she immediately made a choice to sacrifice for my sake. She decided to send me to one of the best schools in the area and used every dime of her money so I would be eligible.

I still marvel at the sacrifices my mother made so that I would have a chance. She gave away many opportunities for herself. She would never let me settle for less than the best she could provide for me. Unfortunately, I didn't always appreciate it.

For me to go to this school, we all had to make sacrifices. I slept on a mattress on top of cinderblocks. We didn't even have a couch, but this was just like Bel-Air to me. The only catch in this middle-class neighborhood was that it would be dominated by whiteness. And I hated it. Being stuck in this bubble, away from all the things I was accustomed to and loved, felt like hell to me. I begged my mom to let me transfer schools so I could be nearer to my culture, to people who looked like me. I had "assimilation blues." I didn't know to take advantage of the environment and the great privilege she was offering to me.

I just hated being there. I wasn't used to the high standards or their academic rigor, so they placed me in special-ed classes because I wasn't up to speed with the rest of the students. I was miserable, failing all my classes, and clinging to the few Black students I could identify with. We were suspended for fighting and almost kicked out of the school for our actions. Those other Black students held the same resentment I did.

What pulled me out of my funk is the special exception I received to join the basketball team. My mom talked to the counselor and the coach to let me channel all this negative energy into something positive. With my track record, I shouldn't haven't been there, but there I was on the team with four Black teammates in an all-white sports program. When it came to working together for the common goal of winning on the court, our interactions were like a movie.

The coach played a culturally white mashup of music from Bon Jovi to the Eagles to country music. In this relaxed atmosphere, I learned about white culture. And my Black teammates and I introduced the white players to hip-hop artists other than the mainstream ones they were used to hearing. I would catch rides with the white players and talk about life. Because of the clear distinction between our lives, they weren't really my friends, but spending time with them provided moments of clarity.

I also learned how to manage being different as a Black man. Being different could get you picked on, but being just different enough can be an advantage. If you're just different enough, then you'll be considered exotic. I started to use this to my advantage by assimilating, or identifying as much as I could, with the majority culture. There was hope for me. I wasn't like "those Black people." I was one of the good ones.

I started perfecting this skill in high school and carried it with me into my college years. When I started following Jesus and attended those white evangelical churches, I remembered those tactics. Most of the men who discipled me were white and came from privileged backgrounds. They introduced me to things I had never seen before. Black men rarely had the opportunity to go hunting, and whenever we did we definitely never had the privilege of access to private game ranches. How much money did this cost? What type of privilege gave you access to this level of life? The wealth and luxury were completely foreign to me. I appreciated that. Yet no amount of luxury could keep me from the reality of racial terror.

I've learned something when it comes to racism in America: it will find you. It is a pervasive stronghold that can't be kept away just because we're positive and optimistic. It is systemic evil that is baked into the fabric of our country. Even if you make as much money as you want, live in the best neighborhood, receive the best education, and have the best friends, racial terror will find and overtake you. And if it doesn't, you'll still have to watch it at a distance.

In June 2015 a white supremacist terrorist entered the historic Mother Emanuel African Methodist Episcopal Church in Charleston, South Carolina, to join their Wednesday night Bible study. After being welcomed and loved by the congregation, the man waited until their eyes were closed and opened fire. When the violence stopped, nine members of the church congregation had been brutally murdered, and a nation was traumatized.

I remember seeing the cliché posts from evangelical leaders. They would say things like "Hate has no place in our churches and no place in our country," and "Choose love over the hatred of others." There were calls to avoid vengeance and anger and embrace hope. They said all the right things, but I knew this was a consequence of centuries of silence toward racism inside and outside the church. Countless pastors and ministries had allowed this bigotry to fester. How dare they lecture us on the day after the terror struck? I felt disenchanted because the response to the tragedy was inconsistent with their normal response to our pain.

In fact, the same leaders who cried on that June day and at the funerals of the dead Black churchgoers were the same ones calling me and my peers "social justice warriors" for our social media posts. They called us "liberals" and "Marxists" because we had the audacity to advocate for the marginalized. They dismissed us as heretics and liberation theologians without ever speaking to us or listening to our pain. They jumped to conclusions about our influences and branded us in public for their followers to see.

The American church was late to the party in condemning racism. We were all scarred by the silence and social scorn from our family in Christ. Considering that I was in the process of pushing away from their influence, I felt a mixture of pain and relief. The very people who had embraced me were vicious in their anger toward me without cause. Yet part of me knew this was the price of my freedom, a severing from their "safe list." The cost was brutal.

I've spoken generally about my losses in this period of my life, but they were substantial. Beyond losing a sense of security, I felt like the white American church turned its back on me. I lost thirty thousand followers on social media—in one day. I remember doing a show in Philly where we had always enjoyed an active market of fans. In a place where typically two thousand people were in attendance, I came onto the stage and saw three hundred people there. *Three hundred*? I couldn't believe that leaning into who I was would cause such a stir.

I lost some fans forever, but the fans weren't the worst losses. The worst losses were my friends. I lost relationships with people who were close to me. Numbers weren't the only loss; I also lost affirmation and artistic viability. I lost a sense of hope and wasn't sure who I could confide in. For someone who desperately wants to be affirmed, it was a profound letdown.

I learned in this moment that race relations in America are more about how Black you are not than how Black you are. How far are you willing to run away from Blackness and Black culture? Are you willing to straighten your hair? That's a step away. Are you willing to dress in a way that completely rejects your culture? Are you willing to stay silent when injustice happens around you? Those are steps.

The more you step away from your Blackness, the more the majority culture accepts you. If you're already Black, then the best you can hope for is to be an assimilated Black person, to have your race "erased" as though it didn't exist. Even then they'll know you're Black. They'll just ignore it for the time being.

In my career, people had always rallied behind me when I rebelled. They were with me and cheered me on. I built entire albums and a movement around the concept of rebelling against the culture. Yet when I rebelled against white supremacy, these same people refused to support me and instead vilified me.

I believe a big part of the backlash to my posts was the word *whiteness*. Whenever I used it, I never used it to refer to individuals but to the system of white supremacy that overshadows our whole world. White supremacy is a stronghold, and its consequences are often felt in broken policies and violence.

The Emanuel Nine shooting was sandwiched in between a line of murdered bodies that appeared in the news, which I grew outraged over and eventually grew numb to see. The Trayvon Martin case was the beginning of the disenchantment. I was still under the impression that if I just explained it to my audience using facts and statistics, they would understand and at least respect my point of view. I knew Black culture and what they were thinking. I wanted to be an elder statesman.

I thought the body cam videos would be the clear evidence that convinced the skeptics. I was sure that eyewitness testimony was enough to answer all their objections. I was naive. No amount of words, explanations, arguments, or videos was enough. They didn't want to know. They didn't want to see.

When Michael Brown was killed, white people told me it was his fault for allegedly beating up the officer. When Eric Garner couldn't breathe, they told me he shouldn't have sold "loosies" on the corner. When Sandra Bland was found dead in a local jail, they told me she killed herself, nothing to see here. Renisha McBride, John Crawford, Walter Scott, Alton Sterling, Philando Castile, Freddie Gray, Laquan McDonald—the list of Black lives tragically lost could go on and on. Even the most clear-cut cases of injustice were microanalyzed to provide any justification for murdering an unarmed Black person.

People of color hold the pain and trauma of these deaths in our bodies. We are a communal culture familiar with collectively dealing with our anguish through shared grief. That's why part of me could understand the riots in Ferguson, Baltimore, Atlanta, and many other cities in America. Part of me understood that property destruction would never amount to anything close to the pain of dead bodies and shattered Black families.

What are the long-term consequences of an ethnic group watching their peers being killed with impunity on camera? What is the cost of this collective trauma? We are a broken people. We've spent years trying to figure out how to overcome our trauma, and at every turn our people are stigmatized and told that the problems we face are the fault of our own culture. To some white people, our problems are all our fault.

Slowly I realized that the most important question I could ask myself was not *Does white evangelicalism care about Black bodies?* The more vital question for my soul was *Does God care about Black bodies? Does God see this evil, and does he recognize the sound of our cries?* His children don't seem to make it an urgent priority. They don't seem to hear the screams and see the tears. But does he care? I thought that if he cared I could face down the losses, but I was so confused I even doubted God's character. I was at a place of doubt because I had to unlearn much of my discipleship to get to the answer.

Yes, I knew God cared about us in my mind. The intellectual doctrines were never the problem for me. I could quote Scripture verses with the best of them. I could build a case using fancy theological words. I could sound brilliant talking about how much God cared for his children. But I wanted to know if he kept any proximity to us. Was the God out there real to those who were oppressed? I was used to interacting with God from the position of the privileged. And by privilege, I mean the people who just had first-world problems, who weren't on the margins of society. The people who shaped much of society. I wasn't used to interacting with a God who was close to the oppressed, who advocated for them—God the defender.

At the height of my shifting influence, a national news outlet reached out to me to conduct an interview about my activism within the evangelical church. I was ready to speak candidly, or so I thought. They asked me how I felt about being a bridge between Black Christians and white evangelicals. I spoke honestly, but of course I held back because I was still learning how to be my full self. I was still "code-switching" for these popular audiences. I was still worried about what the people would think. But one Black female theologian pulled no punches.

When for a Washington Post article, centered around me and evangelicals, I was asked about my place in the Christian context, Dr. Christena Cleveland spoke with cutting candor:

"Lecrae is a mascot for white evangelicalism." I remember being aghast at that statement, not because she was wrong, but because it rang uncomfortably true. What I had refused to confront was staring me right in the face. I never wanted to be a puppet, never wanted to be used by others as a tool for their agenda. But that's exactly what happened. I had been used for so long, I didn't know how to establish agency for myself.

That was it. That was a breaking point for me, a moment of clarity that began a long process of deconstruction and moving away from the evangelical traditions that I was discipled in. For years these mentors stressed that I should avoid the liberation theologians, ironically also the ones who were Black. They emphasized that I should be skeptical of the prosperity theology of the televangelists.

And while I don't have to believe in every single tenet of any theological system, I believe we all need to read a broad collection of voices. Women, people of color, global voices, and marginalized people groups all have something to teach us about their perspective on who Jesus is in their context.

I started to expand my reading and listening to include more voices from the margins. I stumbled onto Tom Skinner's sermon at Wheaton College and listened a dozen times in the next week.[1] He was Black and free in all the best ways. I admired his depth of understanding. I watched endless vid-

....
1 "Tom Skinner Urbana 1970," www.youtube.com/watch?v
=bvKQx4ycTmA&t=229s. The message was originally titled "Racism
and World Evangelism" and was delivered at the Urbana conference
in 1970.

eos of Angela Davis and James Baldwin. I couldn't believe they were living civil rights history, speaking truth to power even when it cost them everything.

I discovered Dr. Carl Ellis, Dr. Cornel West, Dr. Chanequa Walker-Barnes, Dr. James Cone, and many others. Though each of them had different styles and approaches, their scholarship helped to shape the lens that I used to read the Word of God. In my own personal life, I listen to the words of Michelle Higgins, Ekemini Uwan, and Dr. Christina Edmondson of Truth's Table and had endless discussions with mentors like Léonce Crump and Dr. Eric Mason. It was as if a community started to organically form around me. I didn't know everything, but I could at least begin to craft a more holistic version of the faith.

I was convicted not just because I didn't know enough about my culture but also because I viewed it as inferior to the white Christian way. When I was confronted with the beauty of the African tradition, I realized it wasn't just culturally relevant to me; it was also a more authentic life. It was a much more rewarding way of manhood, of seeing the world, of raising children. It wasn't a better life because it was a superior way of living; it was a better life because it was true to who I was created to be. I believe that we are all one family in Christ despite our ethnicity, but each of us has unique distinctions and gifts. That's how God desires us to live. To say we don't see color is to say we don't see the beauty of that diverse kingdom.

I was created to be my fully embodied Black self in my walk with Jesus. I know this will offend other people. They believe that God doesn't see color. Or that ethnicity doesn't matter. They will say that I am radicalizing the gospel and creating barriers to believing in Jesus. But this ignores the ways the gospel has been racialized for centuries. For years I assumed that I needed to fit into a model of what other people expected from me so I wouldn't offend them. It took time and pain to realize that was a futile pursuit.

I found that while some of my Black brothers and sisters couldn't stomach my rejection of the sacred-secular divide, they almost universally agreed about the presence of racial injustice. Even though they served in white institutions or schools, it seemed like they were mum on the issues I felt so passionately about. At first I was confused, but then I realized the cost involved. They didn't want to lose their jobs and opportunities, things they had no guarantee of replacing. We were all afraid of the backlash, or "whitelash," as one commentator has put it.

In all my questioning, I had to face my own inclination to swing the pendulum the opposite way. I am fully aware that the answer to supremacy is not more supremacy. It's not my goal to make Black people the center of all human history or the center of the Scriptures. Many of my brothers and sisters who make that their goal really just desire to have an answer for the issues they've experienced. Yet I don't think putting us at the center is the answer. Any ethnic group will be unable to fully display the fullness of who God is.

But I do think that God has plenty to say about disenfranchised and overlooked communities. He came into the world as a disenfranchised man, a Brown-skinned Palestinian Jew.

I recognize that American racism is not central to biblical theology. It's a part of history but not ultimately history's centerpiece. Racism existed in biblical times, and it's evil, but it's not bigger than death, which Jesus defeated.

I am blessed to be a Black man at this point in history. I am grateful and appreciative for this moment, but the challenges that my ancestors faced still face us today. The realities of oppression and injustice have not disappeared but have only mutated into another form. I recognize who I am, and I'm grateful for what I'm understanding. I am fully embodied. I'm proud of the cultural history that makes me who I am. I love all of my expression and complication. I choose to love it, live in it, and cherish it.

CHAPTER 5

Make America Great Again?

I was actually here. I kept looking around, trying to keep my cool without having a stupid grin on my face. I was in the White House. It wasn't just any visit, I was a guest of the first Black president in the history of our country. President Obama didn't just shatter the glass ceiling that kept us from seeing what was possible. He accomplished it in style. Obama was inspiring for many of us who were stuck in the grip of white culture. He wasn't just a leader. He was a figure of hope. He was the picture of what is possible when we have the full opportunity to be ourselves. I remember watching with pride as America inaugurated its first Black president. Barack and Michelle Obama represented Black excellence in ways that had been reserved for Hollywood fiction. I was mesmerized by the way they carried themselves and hopeful because his "Yes, we can" message had placed him in the nation's highest office.

While I was at the White House, I had my picture taken with him and his vice president, Joe Biden. When I received the picture, I immediately framed it and placed it in my office. What a moment for me and my family's legacy. The most ironic thing about this moment was that I never could have imagined that I would have been a guest at the most powerful house in the world. It was also a metaphor of how far I had come politically.

Obama's rise to the presidency in 2008 and again in 2012 deeply shaped me as a Black man and also affected all the Black people around me. We believed in him, not as a savior or a messiah, but as an example. We had this communal sense that if he made it, then we would make it too. He made history. We felt like we could accomplish anything if our president was Black. Of course my Black relatives and friends shared my enthusiasm. We saw a Black man become president with our own eyes. What a time to be alive and to raise children in a world that at least gave us a glimpse of how limitless our potential is.

Of course I wanted to meet with the first Black president, if for nothing more than to commemorate the fact that Black people have falsely been shown or explicitly told there's a ceiling for them. This meeting is for every kid who believes that lie, the lie that you can't go further than your neighborhood. I wanted my own children to see that.

But I was feeling self-conscious about celebrating this historic feat in the midst of trying to work my way out of evangelicalism and in the middle of losing fans because of my shift in artistic direction. I knew I had to be careful not to share too much celebration on social media, or at least share it with heavy qualifications ("I don't agree with everything the president says on every issue" or "Regardless of your political perspectives . . ."). Many of my evangelical Christian friends couldn't seem to understand the excitement surrounding President Obama. As a matter of fact, they didn't want to celebrate his election. They mourned it. They questioned his Christianity and his motives. They pointed to his stances on a few select issues as proof that he wasn't God's candidate, or worse, that he was a liar and a deceiver.

Even visiting President Obama was seen as a polarizing choice, and I still can't understand why. It's not like I was visiting a dictator who hated his citizens. I wasn't seeing a leader who was vicious toward his enemies or evil with his family. He wasn't even loose with his words. He was educated, composed, reserved, intelligent, articulate—all the things society tells us we should be if we want to be accepted. I was going to see someone who is an honorable man.

Obama was a magnetic personality, a representation of hope and change for some or a representation of the devolving of the country for others. For the eight years that he was president, he was primarily opposed by evangelical Christians who rejected his presence as their leader.

In evangelical circles the only topic more controversial than race is politics. Pastors avoid making social statements and are greeted with controversy whenever they step anywhere near the political realm. "We don't want to hear the talk about what's happening in the world. Just preach the gospel," they say.

What good is the gospel we preach if it doesn't reach our society? Most people in our country don't have the luxury of acting like politics doesn't exist. As tempting as it is for us to act like politics doesn't exist, the lives of real people are affected by everything that we advocate for politically—our schools, our health care, our economy, equal access to the benefits of society. I was slowly learning this, and then the 2016 election happened.

"Make America great again." What does that mean? After my disenchantment with the church and the pain from witnessing Black death, the rise of that statement caught me completely off guard. At first this celebrity political candidate Donald Trump was a joke to many of us. I thought, *He's running for president for the publicity, right? It's all just a big practical joke, right?* I figured he wouldn't gain any traction, and eventually the typical politicians would take over and bring civility to the presidential race. Again, I was naive.

Beyond the white evangelical reaction to Obama's presidency, I was most surprised at how polarized our nation had become. The people who didn't want Black people to talk about politics suddenly felt free to advocate on behalf of this candidate and his movement. Our country has always had politicians and leaders who held problematic positions and advocated for dehumanizing policies, but in the modern era, they were usually cloaked. Most politicians had the decency enough to conceal their true feelings behind coded language and "dog whistles." Centuries ago these thoughts were in the open. Now they were out in the open again.

I remember seeing the crowds grow at Donald Trump's rallies and Christians slowly warming to the idea of him being our leader. He kept talking and being loose with his words, and the support grew. The more airtime he received, the easier it was to see that he was spreading vitriol and making reckless statements. He said what about a Black woman? What did he call his political rivals? This leader seemed to be the opposite of everything I respected about President Obama. I was in complete disbelief. Make America great again? For who? I couldn't believe what I was hearing.

What makes America great, and what did we need to experience again? Sure, some things have changed in positive ways in our nation, but what about the past is appealing to people of color? Even without the full understanding of history and systemic racism, I knew that this country was guilty of heinous acts or, at the very least, looking the other way while they happened. From the Native American genocide to slavery to Jim Crow culture to World War II internment camps to the civil rights movement and many more periods of our history—what was "great" about those?

In the middle of the 2016 election cycle, I performed at a concert in a Midwest city. I was shocked to walk in and see Trump 2016 bumper stickers and signs everywhere near the venue. It wasn't just the support that surprised me; it was the intensity of the support, like he was speaking their language. Where I lived, in a majority Black city, it was rare to see Trump shirts or red MAGA hats. Now I saw the truth of what most Christians, even my fans, supported. I was confronted with the reality that I was going to be performing as a tattooed Black man in front of people who supported Donald Trump.

My issue was never that people believed differently than I did. In a diverse society, Christians will come to different conclusions based on their life experience or political priorities. But I wasn't prepared to see how many people supported Trump. I expected more people to vote for third-party candidates or even to break with the Republican Party because of their distaste for this leader.

I also naively believed that more people listened to the voices of Christians of color. Leaders of color were all saying the same thing. We were all consistently expressing the pain of seeing Donald Trump's perspectives glorified by our white Christian family members. We were crying out to our brothers and sisters, "Do you see us? Do you see yourselves?"

Throughout Trump's campaign, people of color expressed concerns about his language and the framing of his slogan. From the idea of "the good ole days" to the calls for "law and order," his words sounded familiar to many of our elders who lived through the vicious treatment that took place prior to and during the civil rights movement. And in the face of his behavior, many of us made the decision that it was time to speak out.

I remember following ESPN when they broke the news that Colin Kaepernick, a former Super Bowl quarterback, was caught sitting on his team's sideline during the national anthem before the game kicked off. The initial reaction was confusion, but after the game was over he provided clarity.

"I am not going to stand up to show pride in a flag for a country that oppresses Black people and people of color. . . . To me, this is bigger than football and it would be selfish on my part to look the other way. There are bodies in the street and people getting paid leave and getting away with murder."[1] Kaepernick would face consequences for his actions, but for those few minutes everything stopped. There is nothing more empowering than seeing a Black man like me being free in front of the whole world.

I was completely in awe of how bold he was, in the same way that I'm surprised when kids try their parents in public. I thought, *Is he . . . allowed to say that*? Kaepernick was a star athlete in one of sport's most popular positions, quarterback of an NFL team, putting everything he had worked for on the line. He was fierce and unrelenting. He would quote civil rights leaders before him with fists raised above his afro.

After Kaepernick sat during the anthem at his next few games, he switched his protest to taking a knee at the advice of a fellow military member and former player. The kneel was now the universal symbol of protest of an unjust system. It was a rallying cry for men and women of color who could say something, anything, about the oppression that we face on a daily basis.

"He's disrespecting the flag! He's spitting in the face of the military! My son died for this country, and he's disrespecting his memory," some complained. Considering the way people responded when I said, "Black lives matter," I could expect the hatred. Just like activist athletes who came before him, Kaepernick stepped into a hornet's nest, and the

....

1   "Colin Kaepernick Explains Why He Sat during National Anthem," NFL.com, August 27, 2016, www.nfl.com/news/colin-kaepernick -explains-why-he-sat-during-national-anthem-0ap3000000691077.

public's resentment jumped out to meet him. Every single post I made that even referred to him was overtaken with ignorant comments and vitriol, simply for referencing the situation. At one point I was fed up and tweeted, "Take a knee, people riot. Take a bullet, people quiet."

Society's inability to understand Kaepernick's argument was the most frustrating part of the public debate. Why did they believe Black people have hatred for the military? What would we gain from that? I went to Kuwait and other places overseas, performing for military service members and bringing hope. Just like many other Black families in our country, some of my family members fought and died for the freedoms we enjoy. Why would I be disrespecting their contributions to my freedom?

Eventually valuable time and energy are wasted on these discussions. Rather than addressing the true object of Kaepernick's protest, oppression of Blacks in America, advocates feel forced into explaining what we mean when we say every phrase. I'm learning that it's impossible to explain things to people who are committed to misunderstanding you. Much like saying, "Black lives matter," the discussion around Kaepernick was frustrating because it turned into a battle of semantics.

But this type of argument was part of a broader Christian trend when it came to politics. I was learning that even the clearest articulation of the issues would not be heard with charity because it didn't fit the evangelical talking points.

As I grew in consciousness about my Blackness and how God created me, I started to be more open to political realities, but this was a new posture for me. Before 2016 I was politically apathetic. I was under the impression that just like in Sunday school, "Jesus" was always the right answer in political discussions. As a matter of fact, why are we even concerned with politics to begin with? Stop getting so wrapped up in the Red and the Blue and get wrapped up in the Bible. Jesus for president! Because of this simplistic approach to political discourse, I wasn't even fully informed about what the presidential candidates believed.

The last few years have been especially painful for people of color like me who are reassessing our place in the Christian political conversation. Typically the evangelical perspective on politics and national policies has revolved around just picking a few issues that we highlight as explicitly biblical. These issues are almost always exclusively abortion and rights for LGBTQ+ people groups. If you're a Christian, you will not just agree with the conservative stances on these matters, but you'll also vote only for candidates who agree with those conservative stances.

For Christians these issues are so important that I felt ashamed for even considering voting for anyone other than a conservative Republican. I was indoctrinated to feel cultural pressure to believe that there was only one way to view these issues. If you don't vote for a Republican, you're endorsing everything that the liberal Democrats support. And that makes you less of a Christian.

But this was different from how I was raised. I was raised to feel that, as members of a marginalized community, we're also supposed to care about the marginalized and disenfranchised. I felt like the church was implicitly telling me that the most important issue was abortion, so I became a mouthpiece for that. Despite making videos about my own personal history with abortion, I always sympathized with the women who had to make impossible choices about their babies and the quality of life they would be born into.

Do I agree with terminating a life? If you blanket it like that, of course not. But if a mother is on her deathbed and the doctors pose the choice of the baby's life or her life, does she have an option? Can she choose to save her own life and still be in good moral standing? Is she condemned? Better yet, what would you do? Does your theology have a category for that?

In recent years I've been introduced to another group of Christians who are deeply concerned with social justice and concern for the poor. There's a way of interpreting the Scriptures to say that God has a preferential option for the poor. Proponents of this view are not evangelical in the sense of presenting the gospel verbally, but they feel that government policies should be geared toward considering those who are on the underside of our society.

Other of my Black Christian friends would step away from both groups. They believe in morality and the synthesis of the gospel in their daily lives, but they also believe that God is not just concerned with souls but also bodies. In their political morality, education, health care, economics, and criminal justice issues are high on the spectrum, and they believe that the candidates that best represent these perspectives are Democrats. But their votes have never been about full allegiance to a political party; they just recognize that there isn't a reason to vote against themselves if their white Christian counterparts refuse to do the same thing. And many Christians of color feel the shaming of being told that if they have these concerns, they don't equal the concerns emphasized in conservative circles. We are told to pick what's "most important."

I have found myself in between these three groups, trying to understand the value that each one brings without slipping into passivity. I believe every Christian needs a strong dose of nuance and understanding when it comes to the diversity of Christian political perspectives. The problem is that understanding others from different cultures is hard work, and most of us don't want to do that work.

One of my lifelong dreams was to visit Paris. It's a legendary city filled with art and some of the world's greatest monuments. I thought I would have an incredible time, but as soon as I arrived, I realized that no one spoke English. Now, I was prepared for some of the people to exclusively speak the national language, but didn't someone know English? The people who advocate for your visit don't tell you that to fully enjoy the city you need to learn at least some French.

I was a bit frustrated because I couldn't fully enjoy the places I wanted to visit or order food at restaurants with any level of confidence. I could learn a few words and phrases, sure, but the learning curve was too high to get over in such a short period of time. So instead of enjoying the city, I just wanted to go home. I didn't get the fine dining experience there because I went to the fast-food, Americanized restaurants instead.

My friend Bryan actually moved to Paris to work with a church ministry. He immersed himself in the culture and language because he loves the people there. He took time to decide what places he should visit and learned the French way of life. Because of his commitment, he is an effective minister there. But I didn't have Bryan's commitment and patience, and as a result, I missed the beauty and enjoyment of another culture.

To me, this is much like our conversation about politics. Our political discourse is drenched in privilege. Most people don't feel like they need to understand and embrace the nuances of other sectors of society because their lives aren't directly affected by them and because they don't have a theological category for seeing some issues as being important to God and their neighbors. They want too much Black and white when there's beauty in the gradients of color.

Watching your peers die in the streets causes you to believe that police brutality and criminal justice reform are urgent issues. When your kids reach a certain age, the quality of their education and the safety of their schools become very important. When you don't have health care, candidates who promise health care become very attractive.

When people argue about issues that affect people of color, I'm always wondering, *How much does this really affect you? Do you have skin in the game? Do you even live near or in relationship with people of color who give perspective to this issue? If not, why are you so upset about my feelings?*

I believe that Jesus would be addressing important issues that affect every sphere of life. What are the most important political issues? All of them are deeply important to God. Children separated from their parents at the border are just as important as the woman about to have an abortion or LGBTQ people facing bigotry. Your answer will largely depend on your perspective. Are you the parents of the young woman about to have an abortion? Are you the person who is facing discrimination? Your perspective often depends on your proximity. Political privilege is the ability not to care about certain issues because they don't directly affect you or because you don't have categories to explain them.

One of my friends videoed a group of teenagers on the sideline of a soccer field, demonstrating this concept of political privilege in vivid detail. He lined them up as if they were about to run a race toward a finish line on the other side of the field. They were all lined up at the same starting line. But then he told this group to take steps forward if they had certain life situations and scenarios, such as two-parent homes, parents who had a college education, families that were free of substance abuse, incarceration, and so on. At the end of the exercise, many of the Black students were far behind the white students, showing the clear divide we still face and the advantages that privilege provides to run the race of life. If one group can be so far ahead of another in their respective starting lines, how will we ever achieve equity? These starting places affect our proximity to the issues we fiercely argue about.

When I first started making music, I had no idea about this intermarriage of faith and politics that existed in the American church. I didn't feel that the church explicitly imposed its political views on me, but they were unwritten rules, assumptions that started to become louder as the 2016 election approached. I hadn't realized that crossing over into white Christian audiences also meant that I was subject to adopting their politics as well. The Christian music industry subculture is run by conservative Christians. Tour managers, presidents of Christian country music record labels, advertising and public relations directors, programming directors of radio stations, and other key tastemakers are generally conservative Christians. They control the money and power that gives artists the exposure necessary to reach new fans.

Black people who speak about politics are never able to escape the sting of consequences. Society doesn't appreciate the free expression of Black opinions and often responds with violence. Ruby Bridges was the first African American child to desegregate all white schools in a Louisiana town and was greeted with riots and hateful protests. Fannie Lou Hamer organized support for voting rights in Mississippi and was brutally assaulted by the police in her city. Medgar Evers dared to organize his community and was shot dead in his own driveway, just steps away from his wife and kids. Malcolm X and Dr. Martin Luther King Jr. faced the same fate for their prophetic boldness.

Simply because I spoke out on social media I faced death threats. I was called every slur that applied to me by online trolls, as well as being called a "race baiter" by fellow believers. Threatening letters were sent to my house, violating the most private parts of my life. I had no idea that the consequences for speaking out would be so severe.

My whole world was drenched in conservative Christianity—my kids attended a Christian school, and my wife's friends were conservative Christians. Over 130 people left my church after my pastor began to heavily address the ills of racism, and I didn't know how they felt about me anymore. I questioned whether I was welcome or belonged or even wanted to be at the major festivals and among the people who controlled those places.

I've learned that even with this connection of faith, people still don't want you to speak about "politics." To them, to speak about anything that relates to race and current events is being partisan and biased. I don't think speaking about the value of Black life is partisan. I'm just tired of Black bodies lying dead in the streets. I don't think speaking in lament of gun violence is taking a partisan stance. I'm tired of turning on the news and seeing school shootings. I don't think speaking about the criminal justice system is partisan. I'm just expressing frustration for the millions of Black families that are affected by this unjust system.

My hope is that my white fans will consider the depth of their own privilege. They have in front of them an opportunity to use their influence to create more just, equitable systems and to prioritize voices of color. I hope that they enter into our shared experiences with solidarity and humility. I also hope that they begin to do the hard work of discipling and learning to discuss issues in nuanced, thoughtful ways.

I deeply feel the pain of my Black fans and people of color. They are under siege every day in a culture and a church that have proven hostile to their very existence. Amid my downward spiral, I realized I was losing all hope in anything ever changing. While these feelings may manifest outward evidence, I didn't realize how they were changing me. My friend Dr. Mika Edmondson challenged me when he said, "Don't let the hypocrisy of one group lead you to embrace the hypocrisy of their counterparts."

I feel the same frustrations as every other Black person in America when confronted with political dog whistles and when nationalism is put ahead of our humanity. Simultaneously, when I am spiritually and emotionally healthy, I have to think about God changing the heart of King Nebuchadnezzar in the Old Testament book of Daniel and likewise today's leaders who are actively harming others. I need to pray for the leaders whom I perceive to be my enemies.

I'm attempting to model a stance of compassionate, fierce hope over the easy path to hatred and cynicism. I sank into this idea of despising the conservative viewpoints so much that I assumed that the divide was hopeless. But Bryan Stevenson, author of the bestselling book *Just Mercy*, once aptly said, "Injustice exists where hopelessness persists."[2] I can't afford to do violence to my soul through perpetual outrage. Left unchecked, frustration and bitterness will comprehensively destroy me.

At this point in my journey, this hopelessness was slowly destroying me.

....

2   Regina Broscius, "'Hope Is Your Superpower': Bryan Stevenson Speaks at Penn State Abington," PennState News, March 22, 2019, https://news.psu.edu/story/564964/2019/03/22/academics/hope-your-superpower-bryan-stevenson-speaks-penn-state-abington#:~:text=Injustice%20prevails%20where%20hopelessness%20persists,of%20injustice%2C%E2%80%9D%20Stevenson%20said.

PART 3

FINDING HOPE IN THE MIDST OF CHAOS

CHAPTER 6

Is This It?

After realizing that I was never going to be fully accepted in the church, I felt spiritually homeless. I ran from even talking about church or related terminology because it brought up so many painful wounds and betrayals. I was unashamed of my Blackness for the first time in my career, but that was greeted with hatred from the people who had supported me. The consequence for my boldness was losing fans and followers at an alarming rate. I was privately depressed by the crisis in my faith, disillusioned to the point of questioning everything. I was pressured on every side, and on top of everything . . .

. . . I didn't believe in God anymore.

Or at least I felt like I didn't believe in him. I know, Christian artists are supposed to have faith that moves mountains. We are never supposed to have cracks in our armor. We aren't supposed to show any spiritual weaknesses. I never imagined I could ever be that far gone, but that's the way chaos works. Dysfunction has a tendency to creep up on us when we least expect it. We like to live as if everything is normal, but our discipline and faith slowly slip, and before we know it we've hit rock bottom. I felt trapped in a cycle of bondage. Uncovering the wounds of my childhood left me confused and in pain. I was traumatized from decades of rejection. All I wanted to do was be affirmed by people who loved all of me.

In response to my depression and trauma, I would share my heart with transparency in interviews and at concerts. Every time I was vulnerable, I would be hit with backlash that left me bitter. Sin was the only thing that felt like it could numb my pain. But the sin led to shame, and that shame brought on depression. The cycle continued for months, then years, as I tried to find my footing and rediscover sanity. At one point I assumed the issue was my vulnerability, so I resolved to hold it all in. When I made that decision, I wasn't prepared for the inner storm of bottling up the anguish of this chaos.

I was stuck in this cycle month after month, year after year. Every time I tried to pick myself up, something else would happen. I would get on social media and something would happen, and I would numb myself from it all with alcohol or pills. Feeling like I couldn't break free from bondage was suffocating. I felt like a failure, but I couldn't be vulnerable in my failings. I didn't have the safety I once felt in church settings, but the one place that I knew would accept me was the mainstream music scene.

In the middle of these cycles, the only coping mechanism I had was glimmers of hope, faint moments of positivity in the storm. Everything changed when I realized I wasn't just in a dysfunctional state but was battling depression. For a three months during this period, I suffered from a clinical depression that robbed me of my happiness. A number of things caused this pain. Sure, some of it was my trauma history. Some of it was the demands of my work schedule. Other parts of it were lingering effects outside my control. But my poor decisions and self-medication only made my situation worse than it already was.

Depression is a taboo topic in the church. Many Christians would tell you that mental illness is something that can be overcome with theology or just by praying the right prayer. Certain church denominations build their followers up to believe that they can overcome depression if they just have enough faith, if they put the right amount of money in the offering bucket. When those strategies don't work, the depressed sink even deeper into the hole of darkness. When all the tactics they've tried have failed, they lose their sense of hope.

A lack of attention to mental health is a problem in every corner of the church. Reformed theologians tend to interact with their minds so much that they don't have categories for their emotions. Charismatics tend to focus on emotions so much that they ignore the importance of studying the brain. These are generalizations of course. I'm speaking broadly, but the road of discipleship is littered with broken souls, ripped apart by their fear to face depression with compassionate hearts. When you don't hear sermons or illustrations about trauma, you lose hope that people care, even that God cares. My pain was overwhelming me, and I had bought into the lie that I had to figure it out myself.

Many people have asked, "What does it feel like to be clinically depressed?" Every person's situation is different, and I can only speak for myself. But it was hell. Darkness overtook my mind and infected every relationship I held dear. I didn't know what happiness was anymore. Activities that would normally bring me joy only left me feeling life-less. It's like a movie scene when a superhero has all their power sapped from them by the villain. I couldn't fight it off. Nothing was working.

I would sit in front of the television and watch a season of a sitcom and never crack a smile, never chuckle, never respond. At first I kept up the appearance of normalcy for my kids. I conjured up some weak smiles from my reserves of happiness. That worked for a while; then it didn't. Days turned into weeks, then weeks built up into months. What made depression so difficult for me to fight was the lack of rest. *Where can I go to get away from this pain?* I wondered. The studio used to be my safe place, but my lyrics were shal-low. I thought I could work my way through it, but that was counterproductive. Working led to more despair and feelings of inadequacy. *What about the stage? The stage is the cure, right?* Like an athlete who needs to play their sport to block out the noise of their problems, I wanted the stage to be my sanctuary. It never lasted. The moments were short-lived, and everyone expected me to be "on."

I wonder what the pictures with my fans looked like dur-ing that season. Could they tell there was a vacuum behind my eyes, a weakness in my armor? I knew, even if they didn't. The only safe place I had was in the unconscious moments of sleep. Sleep was a safe place for me until the nightmares started. Lucid dreams yanked all opportunity for rest from my grasp. I slept for hours, what felt like days, and still woke up in a fog. Every morning when I woke up, it crawled on me like a dark cloud.

I'm being honest because people need to know that the people they see on social media are human beings. We are weak, flawed, and feeble. We practice the art of mask wearing. We're professional artists and actors for the cameras. While I was consumed by depression, I had to be a "celebrity" in a profession built on a mirage.

The entertainment industry is filled with illusions. Trust me, I know how good it looks. I know how good it seems on camera. But it's not real. What we see in public is an attractive picture of success. We see the glamour, the fun, the adventure, the money, all without the pain and emptiness that follow. We want every bit of the success without any of the emptiness. Fans don't see our messy lives and broken families or the damaged relationships that are left behind from our chaotic lives. As much as I knew the industry wasn't real, I craved it. I wanted all the benefits. This was the group of people who accepted me for who I really was, or so I thought.

I'm lifting the veil surrounding the industry because I had to learn these things the hard way. For years I thought my message would reach more people just by being in rooms with big celebrities. And of course it did reach people, and

God used it to change lives. In many ways it worked. But what does it mean for something to "work"—to experience the achievement of accomplishing goals or to actually be a healthy man at the end of the mission? The more I saw the reality of celebrities' lives behind the scenes, the more I saw how unfulfilled they were. I was one of them.

Their lives were still enticing because they offered me a measure of affirmation. They approved of me. At the time, my single "Blessings" blew up. It was in heavy circulation on the radio. Whenever I would go to a club for an event or an appearance, the song would be playing in the background. People loved my music. This was everything I wanted, right? The applause of my fans was intoxicating, and the approval of my peers was everything I wanted. I thought this was love.

The celebrity world treated me like I was one of them. They would buy me rounds of drinks and celebrate my accomplishments. I finally had real cheerleaders. In this world there was unfettered honesty. Well, almost. The celebrity version of honesty is actually a form of honest hedonism. Once you reach a certain platform, you can say and do whatever you want, for better or for worse. I didn't feel like I could trust my online fans or the church anymore, but these VIP sections were the place I could actually be myself. Ironically, these were the same places that gave me access to self-medication. The drinking, the flirtation, the numbness.

I was at the peak of my mainstream career, and at the same time I was deeply sick. I was finally seen as a mainstay at all my favorite industry events and tours, and as depressed as I felt, it was still exciting to take my family and friends with me. I attended the Essence Festival in New Orleans and took some of my cousins with me. They were excited to hang with me for the weekend and to gain access to all the special events.

In one of the evening sessions, I was the opening act for comedian Kevin Hart in the Mercedes-Benz Superdome. I got chills as thousands of people cheered for my music. I had performed in front of large crowds for my entire career, but this was different. Essence has always been one of the premier Black entertainment festivals, and these were *my* people. They were the ones who understood all the pain I had been through trying to identify with my authentic Black self. These were the churchgoers who were sick of the hypocrisy they saw in the pews. Thousands of people. This was the mountaintop. Finally, I would be fulfilled—a surreal feeling for a man who desperately wanted affirmation. Whatever my soul lacked, these venues had it in droves. I was on top of the world.

After the event, Kevin hosted a private party for the artists and his friends. I took my cousins to the venue with me. Sitting in the VIP section and looking around at all the people drinking past their limits, I just sat there. It was as if everything slowed down, and I really took a hard look at where my life was. I thought this was everything I wanted. I thought this would keep my empty tank filled up with joy. But in that moment, the only thought in my head was *Is this it? Is this all I have to look forward to for my life?* I was happy for my moments on the stage, and I had a lot to be thankful for. But I was still dangerously depressed. Nothing could bring me feeling. The alcohol didn't leave me numb enough to dull all the pain.

The scenario reminded me of Psalm 73:2–5:

> But as for me, my feet had almost slipped;
>> I had nearly lost my foothold.
> For I envied the arrogant
>> when I saw the prosperity of the wicked.
> They have no struggles;
>> their bodies are healthy and strong.
> They are free from common human burdens;
>> they are not plagued by human ills.

To make matters worse, during the cycle of depression, I was spiritually malnourished. I didn't even know what to believe about God anymore. I stopped maintaining any regular pattern of devotion. My life didn't have any rituals of spiritual practices. What for? I didn't feel anything anyway. I stopped being attuned to where my heart was. The depression was dangerous, but my spiritual condition was deadly.

Depression is a serious issue. It drained my life of meaning and worth, but if I could feel anything spiritually, I would have been able to fight it. If I had any spiritual depth, I could have at least fought back or tried to figure out my next steps. People don't understand how much spiritual darkness makes depression worse. The mental illness is bad enough by itself, but when you're spiritually malnourished, the only thing you have left to rely on are your physical senses. If I can't feel anything spiritually, I'll try anything to feel with my five senses. I want to taste something that will blow my mind, touch whatever is going to make me feel good, see whatever causes my mind to fantasize the most—and the cycle continues. I just wanted to feel alive.

That's the real reason so many people spend money on things they don't need, ride the roller coaster of casual sex, or party every weekend until they can't think straight. They just want to feel alive. I learned the hard way that you can't sin your way out of suffering. In the end you just create more suffering from your sin. You can't wake yourself up from a depressive funk with obsessive addiction. It won't work. Trust me, I've tried it. Winning at work won't be enough. The applause of others won't fulfill you. It will haunt you in your private moments.

What a lot of people learned in private I had to learn the hard way in public. My battles were fought in front of the world. My identity was attacked, and my faith was in crisis. I was trapped in the bondage of despair, and this entire cycle was happening in front of the world. I had no private place to wrestle with my pain. People were expecting me to be at my best when I was at my worst.

I didn't feel like I could go to God. I didn't think he cared. I figured he was preoccupied with other things or just not speaking to me anymore. Or maybe he just wasn't real. This cynicism had been years in the making after I thought the pinnacle would satisfy my inner longings.

My journey with God grew more complicated. All my default moves weren't working, and I didn't have much hope that my love for God would come back. I was holding on to that bit of hope, because if my faith changed, who would I be? I threw out some prayers and read a few Scriptures occasionally, but my faith was nothing like when I first started following Jesus. It wasn't even anything like the years before the depression. I couldn't get through.

That year I went on tour with Jill Scott, performing a series of shows and furthering my connections in the mainstream world. That week I had been crying out to God for a sign, for him to show me something, anything that would remind me he was real. Before one of my shows, I was praying for something that I could feel, touch, interact with, some sign that he hadn't completely left. When I finished praying, I felt empty. That was it. If God didn't speak to me or show me something, I was ready to move on from him. I had no logical reason for deciding why that night was the right one. I was willing to do anything at that point. For the first time in a long time, I thought about leaving the faith.

What would it look like for me to become an agnostic? I thought that, sure, there may be a God. I'd even felt his presence before, but there was no telling if that was really God or the conditioning of my religious group. What would it look like for me to become a Muslim? I didn't consider this for too long, but not because it wasn't temporarily appealing. Discipline and love for their culture was always a marker of their religion. What was truly appealing was joining the Eastern Orthodox movement. That choice seemed logical and even made more sense for my deconstructing mind. I should just leave all this evangelicalism behind. What good was it doing me anyway?

After I had that internal dialogue and had performed in front of the venue, I wandered backstage and bumped into the tour manager. In our conversation, he told me there was a guy who really wanted to meet with me. His eyes seemed to urge me to take the meeting, so I obliged. I figured it was a VIP or someone with a connection to the artists, so I agreed to give him a few minutes. When I walked into the room, I was greeted by a collared minister with a beer in his hand. He held out his hand and introduced himself.

"I'm an Eastern Orthodox priest."

Wait . . . what? I froze for a minute, processing what was happening. What I was curious about was standing right in front of me. We began talking, and I realized that the entire purpose of this conversation was to introduce me to the tenets of his faith. *Huh? Is this a test? Is God calling my bluff?* I wondered.

The priest went point by point, and I was speechless. It was as if God heard my prayer and said, *Here you go. See if this is what you really want.* I didn't come away from that meeting ready to follow the priest's doctrine, but it was clear that God was trying to get my attention. He was actually listening. That was my sign. God was real.

These random occurrences became more common. I would meet people who would answer questions I had wrestled with during my depression. Relationships shifted into clarity at just the right point. I would lay on the floor staring at the ceiling, asking God to show me something. One time I asked God, "Are you out there? Do you see me? I need your help!" After hours of researching the faith and reading the Scriptures, I fell asleep, and God spoke to me through a dream. I was stunned. It wasn't an audible voice, but the story was clearly communicating the presence of God invading my life. Even when I was going my own way. God kept speaking to me. He kept showing me how real he was.

That is the most revealing part of my crisis. Whenever I struggled to believe that God was real, he would prove his realness. I realized that part of me wanted to prove that God wasn't real for my own justification, to prove that I had a right to walk away and do my own thing. Sometimes we don't want God to be real because we want permission to sin without consequence. We want an intimate God on Sundays and an impersonal God who looks the other way for the rest of the week. I had paid my dues in the church for years. I went to concerts in small venues, worked hard, went to church, told people about Jesus. I gave God twenty years of my sincere commitment, and I felt like he owed me. Or, if he wasn't real, then the floodgates were wide open.

I was close to the cliff, but I wasn't willing to take the leap off. I wanted to taste the celebrity lifestyle but also knew I wouldn't ever be happy following that pattern of living. I was trying to conquer my trauma by feeling something, by feeling alive somehow. In those moments I was thankful for the contributions of psychology to help me understand why my brain kept reverting back to these expectations.

Psychologists often speak about different forms of attachment that young children experience. Three levels that they normally mention are avoidance attachment, chaotic attachment, and tainted attachment. I had all three levels of attachment, but I was an avoidance specialist. The avoidance stages begin when basic human emotions are dismissed as illegitimate, like when your parents tell you, "Boy, shut that crying up before I give you something to cry about." Or when they say, "You haven't been through anything. Let me tell you about all I've been through." You learn to suppress your emotions, and instead of dealing with them, you are forced to navigate the pain on your own without anyone's help.

Growing up, I never felt free enough to express myself, especially my emotions. That's actually what led me to write poetry and songs. The artistry was my outlet to expressing how I felt. I was a latchkey kid who navigated the world independently. I didn't know what it felt like to probe my emotions. I saved that for my poetry and my songs. It was the only place I felt free enough to be emotionally attuned. I was a verbal processor in private yet silent to the people around me.

Many of us are in a place where we know the bottom is falling out, but we can't put a name on it. We don't know how much we can take before the bottom falls out, so we just find coping mechanisms. Instead of speaking clearly about my emotions, what I found was a collection of coping mechanisms to numb myself from the need to express what I was feeling. This is where I found myself in the middle of this cycle of depression.

Most of us don't know that we're coping. We can't recognize that our obsessive behaviors are actually addictions that empower us to avoid our deeper issues. Then we ignore how serious they are to justify ourselves. We make it through our hardships by any means necessary. My means were alcohol and pills. We assume that the alcoholic is the caricature who slurs his or her words but not the highly functional drinker who goes to work after a consistent hangover.

Even with all the warning signs and flashing sirens, hitting rock bottom was still a surprise to me. I couldn't believe I woke up in a clinical depression. How did I get here? I knew I had been doing some things that were wrong but hey, we're all wrong, right?

Around that time, I designed a shirt that read, "Righteous and Ratchet." It was almost a coping mechanism to show people that I was just a human, not a perfect celebrity to model their lives after. I was saying, "I'm just a human like you." It came across as transparent, but it really was a sign of inner darkness. What kept me there? I'm a public figure. I was successful by others' standards. When you're a popular public figure, people esteem you so much that they're afraid to say hard things to you.

That was the reality for the friends in my circle too. We were all in our dark places and were trauma bonding with each other. I was flailing and figuring out how to navigate my suspicions of everyone. Amid my darkness, God sent men who were willing to surround me. My three closest friends, BJ Thompson, Adam Thomasson, and Tedashii, were my sounding boards, even during the impossible days. I talked to them daily. My pastor, Léonce Crump, was a spiritual guide, graciously pushing back when I wanted to jump off a cliff. Extended family, including Alex Medina, Propaganda, and Trip Lee, helped me to walk through the difficulty.

I *needed* a friend like the prophet Nathan who confronted King David about his sin with Bathsheba, but I only *wanted* Jonathans to join me for the journey. I kept all the Nathans at arm's length from my life. I wanted to work my way through my mess on my own without all my secret sins getting exposed.

I was grading myself on a righteous curve.

I like to relate this part of my spiritual journey to three vessels on the water: a speedboat, a raft, and a sailboat. At this point I felt like I was driving a speedboat, powering through trauma and life with no signs of stopping. When life is great, you're happily speeding forward—until you run out of fuel. After my boat lost all power, I was floating on a life raft, aimlessly being tossed on the seas of life.

I needed God to put me on a sailboat, where he could be the wind guiding my sails. But I wasn't attuned to what I was feeling. I was in pain. And when you're not attuned to your pain, you can't be contemplative about it. You can't go to God with emotions that you don't know you have. You know how to follow rules but not how to pay attention to your inner self. When I made it to the journal, I only found despair. This is what I wrote:

> So, I'm a mess. It's hard for me to see, but occasionally I catch glimmers. I've been grieving the loss of Black lives since 2014. Without consultation, I've been fighting critics and scrutiny since 2012.
>
> I hit a serious low on tour where I saw people so broken and rebellious toward living out their purpose. I was discouraged

and hurt. During that time my cynicism increased, and my faith in God decreased.

I came home from that tour jaded and hurt. I didn't want to read or pray or be around anything fake. I wanted realness or nothing. My friends helped a lot. But then Michael Brown and Eric Garner and Tamir Rice were killed, and it all came to a head. See, to me these young men/boys represented my cousins, my nephews, my neighbors, my family. My heart broke for them and their families.

But when I was transparent about this publicly, many people attacked me and accused me of being divisive. There's a difference between being divisive and exposing the division that already exists.

Then, in the middle of all this, one of my closest cousins was killed, leaving behind a baby girl, then my DJ passed away. People are attacking me on all fronts. With my loved ones dying, my faith crumbling, and my life falling apart, I'm lost. But do I just give up, or do I fight?

I have no strength, I feel trapped . . .

I needed to "open the closet" that stored all my trauma and allow God to pull out my pain and turn it into purpose.

CHAPTER 7

Opening the Closet

Standing in the spotlight is exhausting. Standing in the spotlight without being healthy is dangerous. I was in the middle of an internal and external storm. Actually, it was more like a tsunami. Everywhere I went, it felt like the walls were closing in on me. I couldn't shake the waves of depression and anxiety. I was done trying, done faking it for expectations I couldn't meet. I was done being me.

I was still interested in living but wanted to get away from everything that had dominated my life for so long. Nervously tapping my foot, I opened up my journal and wrote words I never expected to pen: "What would life look like if I weren't Lecrae anymore?"

What would it look like not to be a celebrity and person of interest who was constantly attacked by online trolls? What would it look like not to be cornered about everything I did by people who claimed to be Christians? Wouldn't it be freeing to escape the daily pressures of family, record labels, all the responsibilities that brought me pain? What would it look like to leave everything behind? And not just certain parts of my life. I wanted to leave it all behind. I began to wonder—well, maybe *fantasize* is the better word—if I could escape my current reality.

At first this was just a random thought, a forbidden piece of my journal, never to be read by anyone else. Over time the thought became more than a fantasy. I felt like I could actually pull it off. It was more than a possibility. I wanted to get out by any means necessary.

I wasn't under a delusion. I knew that any exit from a part of my life that so many people recognized would result in taking arrows from the evangelical community, but I didn't care. Fans who had followed me for decades would feel disappointed, maybe even betrayed by my exit, but what they thought no longer mattered. I just wanted to breathe. I just wanted to be normal again.

The outside world never picked up on this. As a matter of fact, I probably showed no visible evidence of the shift. When you stand in the spotlight, you perfect the art of wearing a mask. The word *hypocrite* literally means "an actor" or one who wears a mask. It means to put on a different version of yourself for the masses or your loved ones and rip it off in private when no one is watching. I was a skillful mask wearer, hiding my pain in every interview, concert, and public appearance.

Most artists I know want to make it big. They want to have that viral moment that launches them into the spotlight. Regardless of our jobs, a part of every one of us desires that type of attention. But standing in the light brings heat. The parts of our lives that we would rather not be scorched by the pain of the heat can't be protected when we stand in the light. In time the light will reveal everything.

Celebrity platforms can skew the reality of what people are going through in their private lives. I know it seems like those of us in influential positions are exempt from problems and difficulties, but nothing could be further from the truth. Just because someone is successful does not mean they are free. I was achieving all that my heart desired, moving in all the spaces I had dreamed would accept me. And all I could feel was trapped, angry, and empty.

From the first time fans heard me rap, my whole brand was built around the 116 slogan. "For I am not ashamed of the gospel," Paul said in Romans 1:16. It was tattooed on my body, branded on my soul, stamped on my profile. I'm unashamed. And I took pride in that—not the gospel as much as how unashamed I was of it. I centered myself in the narrative of redemption because it made me feel like an achiever. But at this point I was done being unashamed. It had little to do with the truth of the message, because at every turn, I couldn't get away from God's presence. My distaste for the slogan was rooted in the pain of the evangelical world rejecting me. Even that was just a symptom, but it's all I could think about at my lowest point.

When I hit that low place, I didn't just think about walking away from my life. I laid out the plans to make it happen. No more 116. No more Christian artist. No more Lecrae. I sat down with my business partner, Ben Washer, and told him, "Maybe it's time to pack all this up. Maybe it's time to close everything down and start over in a different space." Even saying that out loud felt freeing because it was an escape from the hell I was in. Why perform for these audiences anymore? Why fake it? For a few months, I silently started making business moves that would facilitate an easy exit. I was making deals and shifting elements of my personal finances so that I wouldn't have to lean on my current fan base to make money. I networked behind the scenes to see if there was a pathway out of the bondage of being me. I vented to Ben about what life would look like without Reach Records and the Unashamed Movement. I was through with my old life. I got to the point where I was convinced all I needed to do was press the detonator button and blow it all up.

At that point I was all done with the public brand, but I didn't know where my faith was or if I truly desired to pursue God. I did know that I couldn't lie to people anymore about how passionate I was. The Christian audience wasn't ready to handle my openness. I just needed to find the right audience. I could shut down my career on the Christian side and slowly, quietly trickle into the mainstream. Surely there was space for a positive rapper in the mainstream hip-hop scene. I wanted to leave behind all the "Christianese" and walk in a space that would accept me more than the church would. Of course, people in the mainstream had problems too, but at least I could be myself over there, or so I thought.

I was so disoriented by the pain that I thought about leaving my wife. We hadn't been on the same page for a while. She didn't understand what I was dealing with, and her patience was wearing thin. The Christian community doesn't accept when you get divorced, but the mainstream world would understand. Yeah, it would hurt my kids, but I would still be present in their lives. They would have everything they ever wanted, plus I would be more relaxed. For years we had a model marriage. We were the example for others, but now members of our inner circle were getting divorced. So how could they judge me? After all, my mother and father had been divorced twice themselves. I was one of the only people in my family to have a long-lasting marriage. Plus I was successful in every area of my life. No one would judge the most successful person in the family. I'd already beaten the odds of the worst parts of my family history. We had put in our time, paid our dues.

I calculated what the fallout would be from others, but at least I knew my family wouldn't discard me. *I'll be fine*, I thought. *Who cares what they think?* I was just ready to be free.

I tried to navigate myself out of my funk in different ways. Of course, I started by following Christian rituals. I was convinced that I could muscle my way out of my issues with my typical spiritual disciplines—reading my Bible, praying my prayers, and studying theology. I thought, *I'll listen to more sermons and read more books. That will cure me.* At first I assumed my problem was intellectual or theological. That's how most Christians react when we're in a rut. We run to those habits, thinking they'll magically fix us.

But when those rituals didn't work, I turned to substances that would engage my senses. I drowned myself in alcohol to numb the pain. I rationalized my addictions by comparing myself to people who I thought were worse than me. "Yeah, I smoke a little weed and get buzzed occasionally. So what? I don't get belligerently drunk. I don't drink and drive. I'm not *that* bad." I'm learning that whenever you say something in your life is not "that bad," you're on the path to self-destruction.

While I was working to prove that my actions weren't "that bad," every area of my life was slipping, drowning even. My musical inspiration was stagnant. My family life was deeply suffering. My relationship with God was lukewarm at best. I had to do something.

In the middle of my mess, I decided to get away from everything. I had to take one last-ditch attempt to gain some sort of clarity. I wanted to give it one last shot before I let everything go. My wife and I booked a trip to Egypt for some much-needed rest.

Why Egypt? Part of me wondered if all this pain was just a result of the corrupted American context. I was consumed with the news reports and the social media controversy. What if I left America and escaped for a few weeks to experience another culture? I was also ready to leave evangelicalism and Western Christian thinking. Having tasted the differences in global culture, I knew that it can be a paradigm shift even to step foot in another country for any period of time. The intellectual in me was happy to see the world through different lenses. The Christian in me was thirsty to see God in a foreign land.

Another reason for my escape was our marriage. We were

genuinely at a point of desperation. The chaos that I was dealing with internally was spilling over into family conflicts and creating chaos, especially with my wife. Imagine watching someone you love drowning in the middle of the ocean, and you can see that they're about to be submerged in this massive body of water, but you can't save them. I was in the moment of sinking, and my wife didn't know what to do. She was fighting to get through to me and penetrate the walls I had placed around myself, but she was at her wits' end. I knew seeing the light would be impossible with all the darkness in our house, so I figured this trip could do us both good. Frankly, I knew that I needed some sort of hope.

Before I left, I had an internal conversation, asking myself, *Is it even worth it? Is it a waste of time to go through all this pain just to keep this life?* Even if I did receive some of the answers to my questions, getting to the end of all my problems would take forever. Seeing the world differently would require all of my effort as well as facing myself. Addressing all these longstanding issues would take me to my breaking point. I figured it was worth one more shot.

Interestingly enough, what was intended to be a time of relaxation and reflection was filled with tension. This was the worst possible time to travel to Egypt. The country was in the middle of political unrest, making any travel into the area dangerous and potentially deadly. We knew some of this before we left, but we didn't know how serious it was. When we arrived, guards clutching machine guns were posted throughout the airport. Security was on edge at every turn. Traveling to our hotel involved countless security checkpoints with more armed guards and bomb-sniffing dogs. *Maybe this wasn't the best decision*, I thought to myself. When you live in the privileged American context, you feel out of sorts visiting places like this.

When we finally got settled, our itinerary was full. We figured it would be foolish to visit such a legendary country and fail to take advantage of the historic sites, so we scheduled time with tour guides to visit some of the key places in Egypt's history as well as in world history. Our first stop was the pyramids. Even in my depressed state, I was in awe of the history and majesty of these wonders. The construction, architecture, and attention to detail were fascinating. I listened intently to the tour guides discuss the history of the region. I forgot all about my problems for that day, completely consumed with all the knowledge. That day was fun, what we considered to be a success.

Later that night the news reported that in between the time that it took for us to leave the pyramids and travel back to our hotel, the exact place where we had visited had been bombed by terrorists. We were stunned and began asking officials if we needed to cut the trip short. Despite our hesitation, we decided to stay, partially because I really wanted to see a historic Coptic church in the city. After the visit to the pyramids, I thought there was a chance that I could feel God again.

At the church I slowly began to drink in the reality of God's presence in the region. I heard story after story of Coptic believers faithfully following Jesus despite outside forces, and those stories moved me. I felt truly inspired for the first time in a long time. God had been moving here long before I even existed. They were an example of faithfulness in exile and under extreme duress and persecution. I saw writings and historic presentations that exploded the limitations of what I expected from followers of Jesus. They would quote authors and theologians who blew my mind. *Why haven't I heard of these people before?* I wondered. They weren't using the same publishing companies that we reference in the States. They were writing from their own unique vantage points.

I was floored by the tour presentation. It was faithful to Jesus in a way that felt authentic, truly human. I never would have known about the books and materials they cited if I had stayed in the West. On one tour a guide showed us a picture of a dark-skinned man who was hailed as a church icon. When I asked who the man was, the guide said St. Mark. One of the foundational pillars of the church was depicted as a dark-skinned man, just like me, in the entirety of his humanity. Whether we walked along the Nile River or toured the historic sites, we breathed in thousands of years of history.

For the first time in years, I saw some proof that I shouldn't completely abandon the faith. I already knew God was real, but I needed intellectual proof that Christianity wasn't just some Western religion drenched in white supremacy. The gospel is a global story, with people from every tribe, tongue, and nation. I felt hopeful that God was up to something. But as soon as we left the church, we heard reports that this church had also been bombed. Again, the place that had captivated me was a place that was visited by violence. We were speechless, but the circumstances taught me a valuable lesson. Ultimately, the place of wonder, enlightenment, and knowledge was also the place that didn't promise physical safety. Sure, it was dangerous to be in Egypt in comparison to where we lived in the US, but our trip taught me more than anything I learned at home. I had to leave the place of comfort to realize that God was not confined to the boxes that my home created. God is present and active even in bombing zones and unstable regions. He always has been.

Another lesson I learned on our Egypt vacation was about the reliability of the Old Testament. The ancient Hebrew Scriptures came alive for me on our trip when one of the tour guides took us to some ruins. The site was massive and beautiful, full of history. Our guide was an expert on the region but had no Christian background or affiliation. She told us about the pharaohs and shared stories of powerful rulers in the region. She took us down the line of rulers until she reached one pharaoh and said, "This one—we don't know his name—but he's regarded as one of the worst pharaohs in this line."

Curious, I asked, "Well, why is that?"

She said, "Because he lost all the slaves."

"What?"

She continued, "Well, they say that he was in possession of thousands of slaves. He was using them to build things, and he lost them all. They all escaped." Instinctively, I said, "Oh, you mean the ones who were freed by Moses, right?"

She didn't understand what I was talking about. She had no knowledge of the exodus, a biblical account that is so common in our culture. Even though she wasn't a Christian, she was a student of history and archaeology. And what she read in her studies proved the Bible true. The guide's verification gave confidence to a doubting mind that was suspicious of everything. I felt a moment of vitality as my mind was opened in ways I couldn't have imagined.

When we're at our lowest point, our problems appear magnified and are all we can see. Our mindset becomes dominated by the pain of the moment we're in. We can't see anything other than what we're facing. But in this moment, I was reminded that the world is bigger than I could comprehend. My existence, even with my fame and status, was so small in comparison to the grandness of God's existence. In the timeline of humanity, my moment is short, and just like other moments, it will be swallowed up in the depth of history. I was so focused on myself that I could not see the grand narrative around me.

I grew up wanting to read and learn everything I possibly could. My desire for intellectual reasoning caused me to have moments of doubt and uncertainty. So, how fascinating that God used my personality to start the process of reviving my soul. He used research, experts, and study to spark my interest toward true belief. And it was the very discipline that I have always been drawn to that caught my attention and provided healing. God speaks to us through things outside our control, and he also speaks through our personalities. Even in one of the most dangerous places in the region, with my mind engaged and my soul refreshed, I felt like I was growing.

Although our Egypt trip was instrumental in giving me hope that change was possible, it wasn't the time when everything went back to normal. I still had much work to do. I hadn't yet confessed all my errors and shortcomings to my wife and friends. I had actually torn down my previous systems of accountability that had been constructed to protect me. I was telling those closest to me partial truths out of fear that they would reject me. I wasn't at a place of confession yet. I didn't yet realize that the only pathway to healing and freedom is radical transparency to the people who love you most.

I wasn't fully healed, but I was in the process of healing. My soul was mending, and I left Egypt with a different mindset than I had before. That glimmer of hope I had desperately searched for was finally present, and I could see the light at the end of the tunnel. I had left home saying I was ready to leave my life behind, but I came back believing it was worth keeping.

Wanting to change is different from knowing how to change. For me this process was similar to how people feel when they get diagnosed with a debilitating illness. Through my work with various foundations, I have had the privilege of sitting with children battling cancer and fans fighting life-threatening illnesses. When people are diagnosed with an illness, they often have an initial moment of despair and resignation. After this feeling, they typically develop a passionate desire to beat the disease and live a long, healthy life. But how can they beat a disease if they don't know the way to do it? As distressing as it is to be diagnosed, everything changes when people are able to see someone else who has already beaten the disease. Even if they haven't fully dealt with their own condition yet, they at least know it's possible to live after the diagnosis. We see this scenario play out in many areas of life. Whether it's fitness, finances, family, or our career, we are spurred on by the success of those who have gone before us.

I was limited by a lack of direction. I was missing the guidance necessary to fully accomplish my healing. But even with these gaps, I did have a few tools that I was familiar with. I went back to the old traditions I learned when I was being discipled. What did I do when I was passionate about God? Aha, I needed to bring back my quiet times. I went back to constructing the same self-righteous structures that defined my early walk with God. It wasn't that reading the Bible was wrong, but I was doing it not to have communion with God but to be accepted by him.

I began feverishly working to earn back whatever I lost in our relationship. After I was motivated to change, I let that passion reach every other area of my life. I started setting up meetings with new artists and spiritually leading them. *No more slipping up if I'm the leader of the label*, I thought. I wanted to show God—no, show people . . . well, maybe show myself—just how fired up I was. If they saw that, they would be influenced and moved to be better themselves. I even applied this strategy to my family. Eager to prove that I was "back," I reinstituted family devotionals and clung to the typical ways of teaching my family unit how to be spiritual. *My family will turn around because I'm going to make sure they do. My label will be fired up again because I'm back to my normal self.* Everything about my transformation was about proving myself, my devotion.

In the middle of this personal shift, I was back in the studio booth, ready to release another album. I started working on the album *All Things Work Together*, ready to show off my new self to the world. Even then, something was missing. Some of the songs dealt with more serious topics, but there were elements missing. My transparency wasn't fully developed. I hadn't taken the next steps.

The problem with my life change wasn't that the actions were immoral or wrong. There's certainly nothing wrong with reading the Bible or leading family devotionals. But the motives of my heart were self-righteous. I was taking every opportunity to prove myself to others, and worse, to prove myself to God. I wanted to show that I was "back on the right track." And this led me to a startling realization.

All this time that I followed Jesus and proclaimed how unashamed I was, I had missed the core motivation of serving him. I spent years being more devoted to my devotion for God than to God's devotion to me. I was committed to loving my service to God rather than loving how God had already served me. I was addicted to my own self-righteousness. It was the root of all my ills.

Everything in life pushes us to perform. Our social media timelines tell us that we're not beautiful enough, healthy enough, wealthy enough, popular enough. We're just not enough, period. Our friends and families have expectations that we can so easily fail to meet. Our employers constantly evaluate our performance with consequences if we fail to meet our quotas. When that same mindset creeps into our relationship with Jesus, it corrupts our hearts and leads us directly to self-righteousness.

Whenever my devotion to Jesus was consistent, everything was fine. When my devotion failed, I felt like a failure. Whenever my actions were consistent with my beliefs, I was empowered. But that couldn't last. My self-righteousness could take me only so far. Without grace, I would only continue to stumble in pursuit of personal health.

I still bought into the idea that I could "be better" and that God would accept me. God had revealed himself to me, and I knew that he was present in the affairs of all humanity and in my life, but I still felt the pressure to perform for him. I still wanted to earn his favor through my list of rituals. If I learned anything in this season, it's that performance can't bring healing. I had to interrogate my discipleship, not to blame myself but to question all my traditions. I thought all I needed was my Bible, my spiritual disciplines, and my performative religious practice.

In American churches there tends to be an overemphasis on constructing a Pauline-dependent faith rather than a Christ-centered faith. We love referencing and speaking about Paul. We home into things he said as if he wasn't a real person. Here was an apostle who was a human being just like us, following the standard but recognizing that he was not the standard. We emphasize the insights into his will and his determination over his full journey with Christ. We often don't take into account that Paul wrote that he didn't want to be disqualified for the prize after he preached to others (1 Corinthians 9:24–27). He was sure that Jesus is Lord and Savior, but he wasn't sure of himself. As a matter of fact, he even said that he wouldn't pass judgment on himself (1 Corinthians 4:3–4).

We don't read Paul in humanity and vulnerability. We say, "Well, if Paul powered through, I can power through myself. I can do all things through Christ, right?" We take these statements to be self-righteous manifestos when really they're self-deprecating manifestos. Paul was declaring that he didn't have what it took to be capable on his own. He was telling us that he didn't have what it takes! He was unashamed of the gospel because *it* is the power of God, not because he was *that* guy. It's not about us being able to do all things; it's about God being the source of every good thing.

I resolved to set aside this self-sufficient mindset. I was done telling God, "I've got this. I'll live up to your standard," as if I could pull myself up by my own spiritual bootstraps. I don't have that power. I was done "white-knuckling" my faith. I needed to leave behind my self-righteous standard and walk into a life of joy.

I came face-to-face with my own self-righteousness and realized that I had lived this way for my entire life. I had tried to find my hope in affirmation and the satisfaction of others, but that was an empty proposition. Even the places that promised unfettered acceptance had conditional limits and levels. There were glass barriers to achieving the favor and status of others in pop culture. I was always working on a way to achieve the highest levels of appreciation, but when I couldn't reach them, I was completely lost.

I had grown up with this mindset in my relationships with family members and in my personal endeavors, and it had carried over into my relationship with God. I was extremely self-righteous with people, keeping score of how many times they failed. But what about when I failed? What about when I didn't live up to the standard I expected other people to fulfill?

I needed to realize what grace should look like in my life. Guilt and shame were no longer the right motivators for me. Guilt told me, *You've failed!* Shame told me, *You're a failure.* But Jesus reminded me, *Your failures are forgiven.*

Believing what he said changed everything.

CHAPTER 8

Unashamed in the Light

was wounded. Matter of fact, I was broken, drowning in the chaos of my own making. I spent years ignoring my own trauma. I medicated through the pain and was addicted to the pleasures of life. And now that had come back to bite me. I knew that I was drowning, but I was finally willing to acknowledge where I was.

When you realize that you're wounded, life has to change. An athlete can deny a nagging injury for only so long. Eventually a reckoning is coming, and ignoring the pain only makes it more painful. I was ready to change, ready for restoration and healing—just on my own terms. The part of change that offends us most is having to be willing to drastically shift our life's focus. But even if we're afraid, we have to adjust our ways of thinking and living to find where we're supposed to be. If we're too attached to who we are, we'll always be afraid to be the person God has called us to be. This painful season of life started slowly shaping me into something new. The problem was I didn't even know what "new" should or could be because of the blinding nature of my pain. I couldn't see what the next season would look like.

Earlier this year every sports fan was glued to the television to watch *The Last Dance*. This documentary followed Michael Jordan as he played his chaotic last season with the Chicago Bulls. Considering our national circumstances, we were all starved for a mix of sports nostalgia and original entertainment. And, come on, who doesn't love watching MJ play basketball? The show was fascinating. I learned things I never could have guessed, including the sacrifices that come with the pursuit of excellence at the highest levels. I was most captivated by how Jordan is navigating retirement.

We all love watching athletes at the highest level dazzle us with their ability on the field or the court. They give everything, and many of them are fortunate enough to make millions of dollars in their careers. Some of my friends are professional athletes, and when I see the attention they get, I realize it's on a different level. Everywhere they go they're mobbed by fans. For some athletes, that type of attention becomes part—or even all—of their identity. It consumes them. They are drenched in the spotlight and eventually drowned by it. Every tweet and post is microanalyzed and critiqued, for good and for bad. But what happens when their career is over? What happens when they retire or, worse, are forced to retire due to injury or failure to play at a high level? They can find themselves asking, *Who am I? What can I contribute to the world that doesn't revolve around my physical ability or the amount of fans I can draw to the stadium?* Their identity is so bound up with their fans that they don't even know how to be anyone else.

Athletes and celebrities are easy targets for us to analyze, but what about everyday people? The stress of performing for everyone else, impressing relational partners, or working to receive applause can drown any of us. We never want to admit that transitioning into health will require us to shed part of ourselves, the false self that was appealing to the fleeting praise of people. What happens when we realize that we're wounded? What happens when we acknowledge that we're broken? When some people reach this point, they decide not to risk that change.

And that decision to stay where we are can permanently destroy us and others around us. Do you really believe that a racist doesn't know that he needs to change? Do you really believe that a narcissist doesn't know that she is obsessed with herself? Do you really believe that an abuser doesn't realize that he is causing people pain? And yes, there are dozens of outside forces that create the conditions for those choices, but we are more aware than we are willing to admit. The change will require removing a part of us that we associated with our core identity. I'm learning that there is no way around this process, no detour, no shortcut, no evading the problem. We either take the painful risk to change the core of our identities, or we will drown in dysfunction.

I was at this crossroad. I was working to achieve, working to be approved, working to be accepted—devotion to my devotion. Pursuing God was exhausting because I only knew how to work for his approval. Instead of believing that

God could override my limitations and mold me into who he wanted me to be, I fell into the lie of believing that I was stuck right where I was. Deep down, as simplistic as this sounds, I didn't think he would want me. Or, should I say, I didn't think he would want the *real* me. I was afraid of finding out who I was without what I had leaned on. At this point I was back to square one.

Just like most people, I was afraid of change. Since I couldn't imagine where I would be if I made the necessary, painful adjustments, I just continued to make up excuses for myself and my behavior. I was asking, *What's a better life? What does healthy look like? How can I even face my wounds?*

Ultimately, my desire for change made me desperate to try anything, even my last resort: transparency. The first step toward restoration was embracing true authenticity. Being *real* is a buzzword for our culture. We're all transparent up to a point, but even that is carefully curated. "Behind the scenes" clips will display parts of our lives, but few people are willing to show all of themselves, and even fewer of us would be prepared to handle seeing those clips. I had used that sleight of hand before, maybe even perfected the technique. But now I truly needed to open up to the people around me, to my wife, to my brothers, to the people who mattered most.

Of course I was afraid. I didn't know what it was like to follow Jesus in light of love and grace without trying to prove something to someone. In my early years, I was trying to prove I belonged to the right "tribe." I was aiming for a target of theological perfection, and it exhausted my soul.

When I transitioned into a different view of the arts and culture, I was trying to prove that my approach was justified. I tried to prove that all my actions in and out of the culture were permissible. I argued here and there about why people should stop scrutinizing my actions, but the proving was the problem.

Think about it like this: Have you ever wanted someone to like you? Your desire to make them like you will lead you to perform for them. You put on a front when that person is around, and you say the right things in every conversation, all with the hope of being liked. Part of this is trying to win their affection, but another part is fearing that they will eventually see the real you and reject what they see. You prove yourself to them by presenting a curated self. You want them to like you but not to see enough that they'll run away from you. This proving creates a dangerous groove of falling into the trap of proving yourself. At some point you will be proven wrong.

That's what scared me to my core. What if I'm wrong? What will people say or think? I'm addicted to substances and alcohol. How will they respond to that part of me? For me to be transparent with others, both publicly and privately, would prove that I was wrong. And being wrong terrified me more than being broken.

When you've been fully transparent with everything that's going on in your world, feeling shame is only natural. You feel shame because all these people who don't know you will use your struggles as the proof that they were right to question you in the first place. Social media will make snap evaluations of your struggles and assume that you were destined to fail because that's what they predicted. "See, we told you that the industry would swallow you up. . . ." It's almost like the parent who dehumanizes you by saying, "You're gonna end up in jail or pregnant just like me." You reject their predictions for a while, and then eventually you give in because you spent your whole life trying not to be that person. Your life can easily become a self-fulfilling prophecy of the pitfalls of whatever it is they believe you shouldn't have done. Eventually that's exactly who you end up becoming.

Over time I realized that I spent far too much energy responding to naysayers, critics, and trolls who would denigrate every small action or statement I made in public. I learned a valuable lesson in this season of my life: I am not accountable to people who do not know me. I should not give them my energy and attention. The arguments will be irrelevant when the lights are off and my family sees the real me.

I had to remind myself that shame and guilt were no longer my motivators. I was no longer working for the approval and affirmation of others, and what people say in response to my story is irrelevant. Whether my life is fodder for cyber arguments should never determine my pursuit of a healthy life. I am a real person attempting to follow Christ in a way that reflects his goodness into the world. I would rather tell the truth and lose an argument than twist the truth to prove myself right. I don't need to prove myself anymore. I am already accepted.

I saw a meme on Instagram of a caterpillar and butterfly

having dinner. The caterpillar looks at the butterfly and says, "You've changed." The butterfly replies, "We're supposed to." It was time to change, for real this time.

I love spending time with my kids. Amid my fog of depression, I began to lose the depth of joy I found in them because of how consumed I was with my own issues. If we pay attention to our children, they can give us energy and teach us countless lessons in the process. One of the joys of fatherhood is establishing family traditions. We have a tradition in our household that whenever one of our kids turns ten, we take them on a trip to wherever they want to go (within reason, of course) with one of their best friends. My daughter constantly reminded us of our agreement, and as that year creeped closer, she already knew which place she would choose. She loves being on the beach and in the water, so she chose Venice Beach.

When she and her best friend arrived at the beach, they were filled with excitement, ready to jump in the water. Of course I had a list of instructions for them, but they were so excited they barely listened to my briefing. There would be no talking to strangers, no wandering outside of my sight, no going to any nearby places, no hanging with kids who weren't a part of our group, and so on. The most important instruction was about their time in the water. "Listen. Y'all can't be going out too far. There's an undercurrent that can take you out to the ocean beyond the reach of help. So stay close." Before I could get out the expected, "Okay, go ahead," they sprinted off into the water to have fun.

Sometimes our kids will test our rules, but my daughter did not want anything to ruin her special trip. She did what she was told. She and her friend stayed close to the beach and splashed each other in the hot West Coast sun. Even though she followed all my rules, something unexpected happened. I had been worried about the current taking them out toward the horizon where I wouldn't be able to rescue them. But they didn't float out deeper into the ocean; instead, they began to slowly drift laterally, away from the point where they started. The shift wasn't dramatic; they slowly and subtly drifted farther and farther down the beach, away from our watchful eyes. Every time I looked down at my book or my phone, then looked back up, they were farther away, not out like I had feared, but away.

I believe that's an accurate metaphor for our lives. No matter what we think, there is no way we will drift toward healthy living. No matter how much we lean on the goodness of our intentions, we will drift away from where we should be. Rather than drifting toward better lives, we will always drift closer to unhealthy habits and stagnancy. The undercurrent of life will take us far away from the place we were created to be. That's what happens when we don't address the issues in our lives. We don't see chaos immediately; the shift is subtle and slow. Then one day we look up in shock at how we landed so far from our destination. Eventually the waves will carry us to self-destruction.

My journey was not filled with drastic moments of failure,

even though I had some of those. It was a slow drift away from accountability and transparency. I drifted away from addressing my fatherhood wounds, away from counseling, away from confession, away from owning my own limitations. It was literally the mercy of God that put me on my knees like Nebuchadnezzar (see Daniel 4). I had to stop drifting, to stop working, to stop everything.

My second step of growth was even more painful than the first. After our Egypt vacation and my cycle of self-righteous white-knuckling, I shut down everything. I knew I wouldn't survive any other way, so rather than drifting even more, I put everything on pause for four months.

Things do not always heal on their own. I have a shoulder injury from playing sports years ago. I felt pain for years but never addressed it. "Oh, I'll be all right. I've got this. I don't have to go to the doctor." Eventually I was forced to go to the doctor so the problem could officially be diagnosed, and I discovered that it was a rotator cuff injury. I didn't want to go to the doctor or hear the diagnosis. Why? Because going to the doctor meant they would prescribe surgery and a time of healing before doing rehab. Addressing the injury meant I'd have to sit back and wait for it to heal. Then I would have to do the work of rehab. Acting as though the problem didn't exist was easier.

Likewise, if I wanted to be healed of my depression, I would have to undergo "heart" surgery, and wait for my life to heal while going through my personal "rehab." Very few of us can stop all working activities for four months and still survive or have a life worth going back to afterward. I know I couldn't have done this without being in my unique position. I left money on the table, canceled tours and shows, shut down all my office activities, refused all media appearances—for a season I left it all.

For an artist, taking this amount of time off from work could lead to the destruction of one's entire platform. A lot can change in four months. You could be in an entirely different place in your career. The industry could move on. The world could change. You could lose a step in your skill. People could forget about you.

I didn't have a choice. I wouldn't be where I am today if I hadn't determined to take time out to rehabilitate my life. The pathway toward health started with me being honest about how unhealthy my mind truly was. And then I had to actively pursue health. That was the hard part. I began accepting who I was in God for the first time in years. I sat with the reality that I was truly loved, truly accepted, truly known. I took long walks without my phone and other distractions, just to sit in a place and hear God speak to me. I wasn't trying to prove that I had head knowledge of theology. I just wanted God's presence, to "abide" as the Bible says (cf. John 15).

As I slowed down, the violence to my soul began to heal. I assessed what I was doing to my body and how that affected my soul. Exercise was no longer an option. I worked out for my mental health, to sweat away the stress of performing for others, to heal from the trauma. The more I changed my habits, the more clearly I could see that my mind didn't need more theological knowledge. What it needed was self-care.

Self-care is a popular term that means different things to different people. For some, self-care is a bath or a massage or an electronics-free day. For others, self-care is just sleeping in for an extra hour. Others can't even afford self-care or understand what it would mean to slow down enough to feel it. Self-care for me is a regular reset from the areas of dysfunction that I've drifted into.

I view self-care as maintaining mental, physical, emotional, and spiritual health. It has nothing to do with luxurious activities and everything to do with healthy rhythms. Random activities cannot overcome an unhealthy lifestyle. I had to determine what a healthy lifestyle was for this season of my life. At the top of that list was seeking mental health counseling.

Whenever we talk about mental health awareness, we must understand that the mind is not the brain. In biblical language "mind" is more closely connected to the soul of an individual. When the Bible speaks about the mind, it is talking about our will, our volition, and our essence. It is the part of us that is making the decisions in our lives. Yes, the way the brain and the mind function are connected, but the Bible tells us to renew our "minds" (Romans 12:2); it doesn't tell us to renew our "brains." So when we're talking about self-care or mental health, we're speaking about the whole self and ensuring that we are holistically sound. If our minds are not healthy, they begin to hinder us from seeing things clearly and functioning as healthy human beings. That's why mental health counseling became a necessary means of self-correction for me.

I owed it to myself and my family to be my best self. The benefits of mental health counseling have been worth the investment. And the only way I can experience those benefits is if I'm honest. Mental health requires self-awareness, the willingness to see destructive patterns and ask for guidance to break those patterns and learn what healthy living can be. Before I could ask how other people would see me on my journey, I had to see myself, and that was the most difficult part. Seeing myself, facing who I really am, not who I thought I was, felt unbearable. But it was the only way out.

Another obstacle to pursuing mental health was realizing that in some cases medication is necessary. Why avoid what can help you flourish? Why run from something that can regulate parts of your brain in ways that spiritual methods cannot? In previous seasons I tried to avoid medication and any sort of prescriptions from my counselor, and it limited my ability to be healthy. When you enter therapy with lines that you won't cross or methods that you won't accept, you're cheating yourself out of health. I had to refuse to give dysfunction a head start before the race began. The goal is not to avoid being mindful or not having to seek therapy. The goal is always health. What does it take for me to be healthy? Is it medicine? Great, that's what we need to do. Is it mindfulness and meditation? These aren't practices to be ashamed of or afraid to try.

Sadly, in many of our churches, we've separated our mental health from our theology. We don't believe we need a counselor if we have a relationship with Jesus. But Jesus and a therapist, spiritual disciplines and therapeutic direction can all work together for our healing. There is no conflict between our mental and spiritual health. In fact, they are interconnected.

To our shame, many of our churches have shunned a connection between cognitive behavioral therapy and theology. What is even worse is that many of the counseling services churches offer are from people who are not professionally licensed. Just because someone gives good advice does not mean they are a mental health therapist. We need to use all the gifts God has given us, including the expertise of those who are best equipped to walk with people through mental darkness. No shortcuts or overspiritualized clichés will work here.

The idea of stepping away for four months wasn't attractive at first. I didn't want to take an extended sabbatical to rest and recover. I would rather have just kept working and figured out my problems along the way. But I knew that if I didn't step out of the limelight, I would destroy everything.

Jesus showed us what it means to be healthy. Multiple times in the Scriptures he stepped away from the crowds to spend time with God, to be with his Father. Yes, there was spiritual rhythm involved in that, but he was also caring for his mental health. By regularly taking a break from his ministry schedule, Jesus was modeling mental health for us. He was showing us that slipping away from all the noise is necessary to preserve our sanity.

During my sabbatical I engaged in professional therapy and learned how to meditate. Therapy was not without its challenges. I desired to have a professional counselor who could integrate all of my embodied self into their assessments. I wanted someone who could see the Black man, the believer, and the artist, and respect all these parts of me. Searching for counselors was one of the most humbling and frustrating experiences of my life. I had initial sessions with a handful of counselors over the course of months before I finally found the right person. But when I found that person, they affirmed my decision to shut everything down.

Therapy became a safe place for me to acknowledge my trauma and process it, which sounds healthier than it feels. Therapy is a place of pruning and breaking. Many times I wanted to evade a question, skip a session, or drop the practice altogether, but my soul craved healing. Every time I left the therapist's office, it felt like my parched soul had drunk a tall glass of water. As painful and embarrassing as the process was, I needed that.

I spent an immense amount of time opening my wounds and dealing with them. I abolished the phrase "no big deal" when referring to my past and felt the pain of hearing those wounding situations opened up from a different angle. I took a hard look at all my traumas and my failures, even how my family connected to my own destructive habits. The key was fully embracing who I was supposed to be as a man and as a human being created in God's image. The amount of work I faced in counseling almost drowned me, but the exertion led to healing.

Beyond the counseling, I closed down my tour schedule and stayed far away from the office, which felt unbearable at first—not because I missed working but because I missed the escape from my true self that I found in the office or the studio. I could hide there and become someone else, and I didn't need that in this season of my life.

My therapist helped me to identify all my stressors and distractions. As I scribbled out that list on a sheet of paper, I realized what was becoming my biggest distraction: social media. Social media was undermining my mental health with comparison and an abyss of arguments. I was so busy debating my detractors that I couldn't see how much time I was wasting, how much my heart was being ripped apart from the violence of others' opinions. I had to leave. For four months, other than a few scheduled posts, I dropped off the map. I even stepped away from television and movies because I needed to keep my mind completely clear of all things that would take me back down the road to darkness.

Instead of my usual habits, I simplified my life down to the few healthy habits I needed to survive. In this season I read everything and stopped Netflix binges. With the newfound time, I set a ritual of meditation at the same time every day. I spent hours with people who truly loved me for me. I spent time with God, but in a different way than I had before. My time with God wasn't on the basis of a devotional or a quiet time. It was just being in his presence, seeing where he led me instead of trying to steer him somewhere.

None of these habits were motivated by a checklist to prove that I completed them. This period was nothing but sincere intimacy with God, developing a true relationship with the Divine. Just like spending time at retreats or family events to reconnect with our spouses or families, I recultivated my relationship with God. Interestingly, the more time I spent with God, the more I realized that he was never as far away as I thought he was. He felt distant and aloof, but when I started to slowly walk back to him, I realized that I was the one who had strayed from him.

The heart that had been full of concrete began to soften. No longer was my experience with God about creating rules or following rituals. I just wanted to sit with God and listen to him. I just wanted to read. When I opened up my Bible, I wasn't studying for anything, I just read until I was finished. Many days that was an entire book or multiple chapters. I fell back in love with reading just to hear the words fall on the soil of my soul. It felt like God was speaking again.

In the middle of this moment, I found God in a different way. I found him in a place of healing, and it was a deeper place than before. It's funny how God has a unique way of meeting us when we're low. The Scriptures say he's near to the soft-hearted and the broken. After every therapy session, in every conversation of confession to my loved ones, in every interaction with my children, I felt broken. And ironically, for the first time I didn't feel embarrassed to be broken. I truly felt like God took joy in me. I knew that he loved the world, but I didn't believe that God really loved me as I was. In some ways I had made God my earthly father who left. Maybe, if I do things right he'll stay, and I'll have his approval. I guess I believed that I could out-sin the cross. I believed that I could out-slide the grace of God. But it's just like I tell my kids all the time: "There's nothing you can do to make me love you more or less." I didn't believe that about God, but in this season I found his radical acceptance. I felt like the prodigal son who came to his senses. "Just give me a working wage. Just make me a servant" (see Luke 15:11–32). God met me on the way back to him. And I was overwhelmed by his grace and love.

Beyond my relationship with God, I was overwhelmed by how deeply my community loved me. I was embarrassed to confess everything to my wife. The pornography that had a tight grip on my soul, the alcoholism that was driving me deeper into depression, the thoughts of leaving her and this life behind. I wept bitter tears telling her all these truths. Even as I said them, I felt a mixture of shame and relief. I could finally tell her everything, no secrets. Yet at the same time, I wondered why she would stay with me after she heard the worst parts of my soul.

My wife listened to every piece of soul bile that I threw up and said, "In spite of all this that you've done, I still love you." She affirmed me at my lowest. She loved me at my worst. She saw me at my most undesirable moment. I couldn't believe I had ever thought about leaving a woman this remarkable.

I had hard conversations with my friends, the men in my life whom I had spent years evading. I came clean about how I was working around my accountability structures, how

147

I had told them partial truths and even wanted them to be "yes men" for a season. Hearing my friends say, "We see what you've done, but we still love you," was overwhelming. They showered me with grace and mercy that I hadn't realized was possible. They saw everything and still loved me.

With the acceptance of my family and loved ones, I slowly became a more empathetic and present man. For years I had been running at a million miles per hour, spending twenty days at a time on the road. It was easy to run from the uncomfortable work and avoid facing myself. But in this season everything stopped. I was fully present at home with my family, and our rhythms became healthier and more consistent.

This journey did not culminate in my four-month sabbatical period. I did not reach the point of conquering every struggle and overcoming every obstacle. That was never the point. The point of growing a healthy soul was not to arrive at a destination. Health is not found in a location; it's found in a personification. Health is not found in a place; it's found in the presence of Jesus. That's what changed everything. The change in rhythms just altered the pace of how I walked, but it didn't change my ultimate location of freedom.

I haven't arrived in life, but I have arrived in Jesus's presence. I'm with him wherever I go. Jesus cares not just about my soul and my spirit but also about my body and my mind.

Once I began to find my way out of the darkness, I was no longer ashamed of my scars. Now I show off my scars to let people know that healing is possible. If we're ashamed of our story, we can't share who we really are. We will never know triumph without trial. God healed me in the midst of my trauma. I had to go through the cocoon to emerge as a butterfly, and I can't just hate what happened in the cocoon. I have to appreciate it for making me who I am.

The chaos didn't consume me. I came out stronger. I changed.

CHAPTER 9

Owning Your Darkness

Spending four months away from the steady grind of being an artist and executive energized me. For the first time in a long time, I was able to be fully present at home. I didn't speed through family rituals but soaked in every moment. I remember sitting in the living room after one of our family devotional times. Devotionals were always sweet and revealing, but this family study time was especially rewarding.

I was sitting with my son after the devotional, enjoying time with him. In the middle of our conversation, he randomly blurted out, "Dad, I wanna be like you."

"What?" I said.

"I wanna be like you, Dad."

Over the past few years, I hadn't been much of a father to my kids. I was present in all the bare minimum ways, but I wasn't fully invested in their lives. I didn't value their words or the quiet moments of family devotions. I was consumed with trying to climb out of my own cycle of chaos.

So this statement from my son was the full circle moment after everything I had put my family through, after years of depression and dysfunction.

Coming from my lack of experience with fathers, I didn't know how to respond to my son. I felt a rush of emotion and didn't say much, just held him close. *My son wanted to be like me.* For that moment, I would have traded all my Grammy and Stellar awards, all the concert crowds, all the positive press from people who didn't really know me. I finally knew that I was growing into a man worth following.

I sat in this divine moment and thanked God. Just six months before this conversation, I had been completely shattered. My mind was a mess of anxiety and self-destruction. My body was suffering from addictive behaviors, and my spirit was drier than a desert. I would have been ashamed if my son said that to me in that season, but now I felt like I had jumped into a hot tub on a freezing winter day. I was bathed in warmth and acceptance.

My son's words revealed that my trauma did not have to be a hindrance to my purpose; it could be a step toward living out my purpose. My trauma could be redeemed and restored. His words helped me realize that I did not have to surrender to my mistakes. As bad as my patterns had been, it was never too late to take a step toward the light. Instead of denying my weaknesses or the things in my life that were hard, I needed to embrace them to become the best version of myself, to flourish as God had created me.

To be clear, I'm not perfect. Growth requires self-awareness, but it also develops it. The more I learn, the more

I realize I don't know anything. Even now, I fall back into the patterns of weakness that characterized my seasons of unhealthy brokenness. All the therapy in the world wouldn't make me perfect. I'm still working to unlearn those dysfunctional patterns that plunged me into that self-destructive cycle. But the habits that were destroying my life are no longer present in this season of my life. I left those behind for a more fulfilling life of freedom. After truly sitting in the presence of God and submitting to healthier rhythms, I finally feel true joy. I feel peace that overwhelms me and drives out chaos when I wake up. I feel the love that comes from allowing myself to be forgiven without constant shame.

Recently I was telling a friend how much has changed in my life. I was marveling at how many unhealthy habits are no longer part of my daily rhythm. From the way I wake up to the speed of my movements, my new life looks nothing like my old life. Even in the middle of the busiest parts of my career, I don't rush like I used to. In fact, to ensure that I don't rush through life, missing the moments, I literally schedule rest in my calendar, not just yearly but monthly and weekly. No matter how packed my schedule is or what I am facing at work, I always try to have daily distractions, weekly withdrawals, and annual abandonments.

The routine of life can wear down our souls and destroy our ability to be present in the moment. Over the years, we become worn down by submitting to the routine of our schedules rather than constructing our schedules to benefit us. We usually make plans considering productivity rather than our health. But what is healthful should always take precedence over what is productive. For workaholics, maintaining a healthy mind is especially difficult. But I no longer let my schedule dictate what I do. I now implement daily distractions into my schedule to give my mind a break. These can be deep and theological, or they can be fun and leisurely. Regardless of what these distractions entail, my mind needs a break from functioning as a *human doing* to live as a *human being*. Scheduling in some sort of mental activity that takes me away from work and the pressures of my job is essential to maintaining a healthy mind.

I quickly learned that even daily distractions are not enough to fight off the desire to work nonstop. As a result, I started studying the ancient rhythm of sabbath-keeping. The Sabbath was designed by God as a day to rest from labor, to enjoy God's creation, and to admit that we cannot do everything on our own. We weren't designed to work seven days per week. No one is designed to be "on" at all times or never to destress from the pace of life. Beyond needing physical rest, I need to rest from the need to "do more." So in our house we work for six days, and then we rest, giving all of our worries about what we didn't get done to God. The Sabbath is on my calendar so I can't ignore it or forget to observe it.

As great as the Sabbath is for developing the reminder that I am not God, I need more. My mandatory four-month break vividly showed me that disconnecting is not an option. I can either willingly unplug from my life and take a true vacation or I will be forced to take a permanent vacation after I destroy my life. The choice is up to me. Every year I plan a vacation with my wife to completely unplug from the pressures of both work and home.

Right now, for the first time in a long time, I feel healthy enough to flourish in all areas of my life. That was one of the biggest indications that I had changed. I slowly crept back into the studio and felt . . . different. My music was resonating with my lived experience in a fresh way. I felt healthy enough to record material that would stand the test of time.

I established new rules for all my public appearances and slowly rebuilt my accountability systems. When I took time off, I revamped the safeguards I had previously torn down. I had evaded the loving rebuke of my friends in the previous season, but in this season I needed to ask hard questions about myself and my habits. The answers weren't found in my new rhythms that would provide necessary boundaries to ensure that this freedom was not just for a season. Even more than never wanting to get close to sliding backward again, I am convinced that healthy rhythms will allow me to actively pursue a healthy, whole life. This includes how I structure time with my family and the regularity of our breaks. Our new family disciplines have brought me joy. They don't always work out how I think they should, but I don't find them to be a burden like I did before.

Routine therapy is part of my new rhythm. I've committed to going to therapy consistently for maintenance, not just for emergencies. I call my counselor not just when things fall apart but even when things appear to be in order. Most of our negative habits start in times of peace, not times of chaos. Because I know what that feels like, I schedule regular therapy sessions no matter how busy I am. God has allowed me to see the benefits of therapy in a personal, powerful way, and by extension, I have a deeper appreciation for all "specialists" in the kingdom of God.

For years I told people that I wanted to be vulnerable, to be transparent for all the people who have followed my journey. The vulnerability I thought I was displaying was always about helping others. I shared my scars because I thought they would provide clarity for fans, not for myself. Now I want to talk about personal freedom for myself. I've talked about my past, but I'm ready to talk about overcoming. I'm ready to talk about living in the light of the blessed reality of restoration.

When I was stuck in my pattern of depression and anxiety, I couldn't even imagine being healthy. It seemed like an elusive fantasy. I was convinced I would be nothing more than a lifelong disappointment to myself, to those I love, and to God. But for the first time in a long time, I feel free. It feels good, truly human, and healthy.

Adopting healthy habits was a key part of my growth, but other factors contributed as well. My mentality had to adjust from working to be affirmed to resting in the affirmation that I had already received. I also stopped believing that "a system" would protect me. Yes, I should establish a holistic approach to a flourishing life, but I am not saved by a system; I'm saved by a Savior. Overcoming in a difficult season doesn't guarantee that I'll avoid difficult circumstances in the future, but the challenge is to approach them differently now than previously.

All my loved ones know that I enjoy listening to podcasts. They are the perfect way to broaden my perspective while I attempt to deal with Atlanta traffic (another reality that teaches me I'm not in control). During my commute to work and in my travels, I fell in love with a podcast called *Ear Hustle*. This audio journey is unlike anything I've ever heard before. The award-winning show provides firsthand accounts of life inside prison and shares them solely from the perspective of those who are incarcerated. *Ear Hustle* also features stories of people who are trying to assimilate back into society after their time in prison, humanizing the daily fight to avoid recidivism back into the criminal justice system. As I was captivated by real stories from real incarcerated human beings, I was infuriated by the legacy of mass incarceration. I saw how the "war on drugs" created tragic conditions that affected Black and Brown families for generations to come. It served as a reminder that I should never forget about them and should advocate on their behalf as much as I can.

I devoured their stories. They were hopeful, insightful, and many times tragic. After listening to the podcast and appreciating the quality of the production, I had the privilege of actually performing a show inside San Quentin State Prison, where the podcast is recorded. Beyond being able to feel the energy of the crowd and see the hope on their faces as they listened to my music, it was a unique opportunity to meet with men who were full of such complexity and compassion. It was a holy moment, a favorite of all the shows I've performed.

The highlight of the visit was being able to talk with Rahsaan Thomas, the new cohost of *Ear Hustle*, about life and his personal experiences. He shared many stories with me. I was riveted listening to him talk about the decisions he made when he was younger and how his childlike behavior ruined his future. He told me that when he first arrived in prison, he was depressed, frustrated, and angry with everything. Entering into prison, knowing you are destined to be locked up for years can lead to hopelessness. He told me that he was in this state of despair for years and was ready to resign himself to his fate. He lived in that funk until he had an epiphany. He realized that he couldn't change his situation, but he could better himself in the middle of his situation. Even though he could not get out of prison, the culture of despair the system cultivated in him did not have to remain. He could learn, grow, and mature.

Filled with fresh resolve, Thomas began reading everything in sight. He utilized the prison library system to study economics and writing. He realized that his isolation provided him with the time he needed to become better than he had ever been before. Slowly, as he began to write, his confidence grew. He shared some of his writings with other incarcerated men and was encouraged by their feedback. Eventually his brilliant work was featured in national publications like Vice and GQ. He had found purpose in the middle of his pain. If his sentence is commuted, Thomas will be released with a writing career and a financial foundation that will serve him for years to come.

I realized that in a different context, I experienced a similar turning point. No, I may not have been able to change my physical situation, but God could change me in the middle of my situation. Now, don't get me wrong—I desire God to change every adverse situation I bring before him, but even if he doesn't, he is still enough in the middle of it all. Very few people are able to authentically speak from that place, but for those who are, there is profound freedom. When situations cannot dictate your joy and peace, you honestly feel unstoppable. Yet the road to that fulfilled place can be painful and costly. To journey there, you must be humble enough to say that you don't have anything else but God. It requires you to reach your breaking point and realize that everything you have is small in comparison to what truly matters.

Life's turning point comes when you are able to admit, "God, I don't like where I am, but you're with me, and that's enough." That turning point was a special place for me to discover. It is a place of surpassing peace and foundational hope. No matter where we are, God is present and involved in every aspect of our lives. He is on the surgery table, lying next to you. He is in the room when your mental darkness won't lift and you have to take medication. He is with you while you're going through chemotherapy. Wherever you are, he is there, and he cares even more about our well-being than we do. Ultimately, in some grander way, we will be better and the narrative will be for our good.

Circumstances don't disturb me now like they did before, because my core foundation can't be shaken. I imagine this is similar to where the apostle Paul was when he was in prison, beaten, stoned, and shipwrecked. In the middle of all his troubles, he learned to be content. Beyond wanting to be famous or successful, beyond the pull of achieving all the goals you wrote down for your life, the most elusive state of being is contentment. When you know that regardless of any situation you find yourself in, you are not bound by that circumstance, you are free. Sometimes it takes everything being stripped away from you to find it.

After all the changes in my life, I was able to find contentment in the presence of God. Without having to know every step of my future journey, I know enough to follow Jesus wherever he leads. I want to be like the disciples, the apprentices who walked in the dust of their Rabbi, Jesus. Wherever he leads me, that's where I want to be.

Beyond having a contented mindset, I developed muscles that I didn't even know I had. We must use each "muscle" of faith and every human tool at our disposal in its proper context as God intended it. I'm tempted, at this point in my journey, to say that counseling is the answer. Counseling is not the answer; it's the provision for my health. Others might think that eating right and exercise are the answer; they are not the answer but the provision. These tangible means are benefits, but they are not preeminent. We need every tangible muscle, but we also need the intangible muscles of spiritual fellowship with God.

In an effort to provide you with more tools, I want to share a few mental perspectives that have proved to be invaluable in this season of my life. These are some perspectives that emerged from my journey of trial and trusting, and while they are not exhaustive, they give me a clear picture of what I learned after coming out to the other side of my brokenness.

The Redemptive Reading of God's Story

The biggest shift in my spiritual perspective involved coming face-to-face with how I viewed the Bible. In this season of life, I read the Bible from a completely different perspective than I had before. In times past I approached the Bible with a transactional mentality. I went to God's Word for what I could gain from it. I would read the Scriptures with the goal of trying to make myself better. As much as I talked about the grace and mercy of God, I wanted to please God by proving my devotion.

In fact, that was the root of my problems. I didn't truly believe in the possibility of God's redemptive story. I only believed that God could redeem me in "salvation," or in the moment when I made the decision to follow Jesus. I thought that he was redemptive only in that moment, not that he could take me from the lowest of low places and build me back up. When you read the Scriptures with this lens, it's hard to believe that some of the stories are even real. They are far away from our context. But put yourself in their reality and you'll find that the biblical accounts are not faraway pictures of a mythical spirituality. They show us just how powerful God's redemption can be for us. Consider these examples:

- Noah was a drunk.
- Abraham was too old to have a son.
- Isaac was a daydreamer.
- Jacob was a liar.

- Leah was ugly.
- Joseph was abused.
- Moses had a stuttering problem.
- Gideon was afraid.
- Samson was a womanizer.
- Rahab was a prostitute.
- Jeremiah thought he was too young to do God's work.
- David was an adulterer (not to mention a murderer).
- Elijah was suicidal.
- Isaiah preached naked.
- Jonah ran from God.
- Naomi was a widow.
- Job went bankrupt.
- John the Baptist ate bugs.
- Andrew lived in the shadow of his big brother.
- Peter denied Christ.
- The disciples fell asleep while praying (and ran away when Jesus really needed them).
- Martha worried about everything.
- The Samaritan woman was divorced five times.
- Mary Magdalene was demon-possessed.
- Zacchaeus was greedy.
- Timothy had an ulcer.
- Paul was a Christian killer.
- Oh . . . and Lazarus was dead.

When you take note of these examples, you start to realize that we don't believe in a God who discards people and throws them in the gutter when they make mistakes. We also don't have a faith that gives us the power to put others away for mistakes. Even the worst of people can be redeemed from their past. While it is inspirational to say that in theory, how far do we believe that God's redemption can reach? Seeing my own mistakes has forced me to answer that question.

I believe that God can redeem even those who are abusive and predatory if they turn from their ways and receive the help they need. That's why I refuse to hold on to hatred of and bitterness toward my abusers. Clinging to that pain and letting it cloud my vision would be easy, but I believe even my abusers can be redeemed.

I believe God can redeem absentee parents, including my biological father, even as I deal with the pain of his absence. I spent so much time running from being like him and being bitter because he ran from me that I didn't realize he had a past just like me. Maybe he needed something that he never received in his own upbringing. Maybe he struggled with trauma and never had the privilege of going to therapy to work through his pain. He made poor choices that affected our family and my future, but even with all that baggage, he can be redeemed.

I have been wounded by fellow Christians who impugn my motives and make uncharitable statements about my positions. Their vitriol has hurt me and still continues to leave wounds that I'm working through. But as much as I wanted to leave the faith altogether, I came to the conclusion that we're all learning and growing. A few years ago, I was just like them with that same attitude toward others. If I can be redeemed, then so can they.

Hashtags and protests reveal countless instances of white supremacy and bigotry from racists who feel empowered by the climate of our culture. Their actions and words are vile, revealing the darkest parts of the human heart. But I pray that they leave their evil patterns of behavior. Even racists can be redeemed by God.

The 2016 election revealed the church's collective apathy toward the marginalized. When the American church should listen, it has silenced our voices in favor of the status quo. We are still reckoning with the pain of the policies that have hurt so many and the rhetoric that continues to dehumanize. But God can still redeem the comfortable and complacent people in our society.

I was addicted to self-destructive patterns of behavior that almost destroyed my life and everything I worked for, but God didn't give up on me. He came after me and picked me up, even after my most embarrassing moments. God brought me out of my pit. Because he redeemed me, I'm convinced that everyone who has fallen short can find redemption.

For years I've heard that "the ground is level at the foot of the cross," but now I actually believe it for myself.

The Consistency of God's Character

In my darkest moments, I questioned God. I didn't just doubt my relationship with him on a personal level, but I extended that doubt to his existence. I don't know of many people who never go through seasons or moments of doubt. Many people have trouble reconciling what they believe about

God with their circumstances, causing them to abandon the faith entirely. After enduring the consequences of decades of trauma and years of self-destructive behavior, I have never been more confident in the consistency of God's character.

I don't say this to shame anyone else's doubts or cause people to feel as though I am a superior follower of Jesus. I can only speak about how what I have walked through has deeply expanded my capacity to believe God. I stumbled, but God didn't leave me. I fell on my face many times, and with each fall his hand was extended to me. He never let me stay where I was.

We often feel like God is no longer speaking to us or we can't hear his voice anymore, but I interpret silence differently now. God is always speaking to us in different ways. It's just that we're locked into one frequency. His Word can communicate to us in whispers of comfort and in shouts of instruction. God speaks through pastors, poets, prophets, and the poor. He uses all of life to show his glory.

I was expecting God only to speak using my frequency, when he was always communicating in his own way. I even believe my dark moments were designed to tune my heart to a wider range of hearing God's voice.

Growth into Mature, Whole, Communal, Global Christianity

The thing that has most significantly altered my daily life and work is the shift to a broader view of my faith. My views of Christianity have dramatically expanded. In the early days of my walk with God, I was the tribal devotee addicted to proclaiming my own self-righteousness. Maybe more importantly, I was convinced that I needed to promote my own "self-rightness." "I am right, and you are wrong" was the mantra for this season of my journey. That brand of faith is no longer appealing. The desire to prove my devotion to others who are watching has completely left me. I am working diligently to pursue a mature, holistic, communal, and global perspective of following Jesus.

For all my knowledge and understanding, my life didn't resemble the meek, mature picture of Jesus. I was intellectual and "theologically sound," but I was emotionally and mentally unhealthy. What good is my theology if it never reaches my ethics? What good is my knowledge if it never touches my actions? I was all about myself and how I could gain affirmation from others. In that season, I was convinced that I was passionately pursuing my Savior, but it wasn't about him.

Mature Christianity isn't concerned with superficial appearances; it is concerned about God's calling. Maturity is humility in the face of private critique and public shame. Maturity is honestly admitting "I don't know" about the countless debates that dominate social media. Maturity is faithful commitment to God and contentment with God's purpose for your life.

A Holistic View of Faith

I also see now how important it is to have a holistic view of my faith. Every area of life cannot simply be reduced to a theological issue. God is not only Lord over our theology, but also the One who uses every other human discipline. I believe that denying these disciplines in our discipleship has left the church stunted and ineffective where it should be growing. This was my experience as I grew in my journey with God.

I felt ashamed to admit I needed help or a counselor, even to my closest friends. While "Pray about it" is always good advice, some people need the help of an expert in the field of psychology or therapy. Emotional health needs to be incorporated into our discipleship. Mental health needs to be preached about in our sermons. We need healed people to tell us how they reached the reality of healing.

We need historians to tell us the truth about the racial and cultural history of our local churches and denominations. We need women to be given the opportunity to lead us in areas other than women's ministry. We need a theological vision that seeps into our politics, health care, economics, education, and families.

Christianity is unattractive to some, not because Jesus is not attractive to them but because we have refused to show how he transforms all of life into a new reality. I want to show the people in my circle of influence that there is a holistic beauty in following a Savior who cares about every area, not just church attendance and spiritual rituals.

Community as a Priority

Community is no longer optional for me. I came face-to-face with my own shortcomings, with the uncomfortable reality that I have no way of doing life on my own. I approached life like I was a superhero, believing that each obstacle needed to be leaped over and white-knuckled through. But some giants aren't designed to be conquered alone. I treated my friends like "Jonathans." If you're familiar with the biblical story of David, you know that Jonathan was his closest, truest friend. David loved Jonathan as a brother even though Jonathan's father, King Saul, despised David.

Jonathans are essential. We all need those people who will be a constant well of encouragement and side with us even in difficult circumstances. We need Jonathans, but we also need some "Nathans." Nathans are the friends who, like the prophet, called out the king for his destructive actions that affected not just him but other people as well. I need people who are willing to challenge me to be better, who call me to account when I'm clearly off base. I need those who see destructive behavior to tell me the truth and not take no for an answer. I need people who are not enamored with my success and celebrity, but above all else desire my soul to be healthy.

After my season of darkness, I found those friends. I had them before, but it was cemented during my darkest moments. These friends aren't simply people I make music with but are true blood brothers who saw my worst and still believed the best. I realized how important Tedashii, BJ Thompson, Adam Thomasson, and my pastor, Léonce Crump, are to my life. I gained a greater appreciation for Trip Lee, Alex Medina, Propaganda, and Dr. Eric Mason. These men told me the truth, continue to tell me God's truth, and listen to my truth without dismissal.

A Global Viewpoint

Jesus was not American. He didn't come waving an American flag or to set up a regime of patriotic nationalism. He came to introduce a new way of living through his kingdom. We need to understand both Jesus and the Scriptures in their context. Context protects us from believing that Western evangelicalism and our theological tribes have a monopoly on the gospel message. I knew that in my head before, but now I believe it in my heart. I don't have to serve the Western construct of faith or the American church's priority of what it tells me is most important. I don't have to listen to the same people just because they are marked "safe" by tribal onlookers. Listening to fellow Black Christian thinkers and theologians has changed my life, but many of them are often dismissed because we would rather stay in our comfortable categories.

Tribalism will dismiss different traditions or denominational expressions simply because they challenge the status quo. We ignore these contributions even though they reflect the diversity of Christ's body. I heard somewhere that the average follower of Christ is a poor woman from the Southern Hemisphere, not a white man or an affluent American.

We need to listen and learn from Brown churches just across the southern US border who are constantly under the pressure of serving migrants eager to find a better world. We need to listen to the African pastors who are dealing with extreme poverty and colonialism. We need to hear the Asian perspective on theological topics and the perspective of indigenous people who have endured generational trauma under Western domination. We need to see what it looks like to value the diverse contributions of all kinds of people in the kingdom of God, not just the ones with power and status. I share these perspectives not because they are the only observations I made during this painful season but because they rose to the surface.

God is making a masterpiece out of my mess. It is easy to believe that the masterpiece is the triumph of overcoming the dark places and personal obstacles, because we think of a masterpiece as a finished product when we see one in a museum. But God's masterpieces are unfinished products.

I look at what I have as a process. The masterpiece isn't the accolades and awards I've received or my personal victories. The masterpiece is the closeness, security, and comfort I wake up with every day, knowing that God is with me. It is having assurance that I have a relationship with God that's not going anywhere. The masterpiece is being able to see the love of God—its depth, width, height, and breadth—and being able to be okay with that as my healing.

To those who read this, wherever you are in life, my desire is that you will find hope in Christ. I found something new in this past season. The brokenness made me stronger than before. Yes, I went through hell, but the fire forged a new me. God is making a masterpiece out of my mess.

The masterpiece remains unfinished. . . .

Restoration

Use your camera or barcode reader
to scan & listen to the album.